MW01243311

The

DOPE

GRAMMAR GUIDE

Vol. 1: The Basics

Sasha Ravae

BLACK EDEN
PUBLICATIONS

BLACK EDEN PUBLICATIONS™

The Dope Grammar Guide - Vol. 1: The Basics

ISBN: 978-0692930540
United States:
10 9 8 7 6 5 4 3 2 1

The
DOPE
GRAMMAR GUIDE

Vol. 1: The Basics

Table of Contents

Preface

When I was in college, I became very interested in how our language functions. I loved taking grammar courses because English became like a science to me. There are rules for every part of the written word, and I planned to learn them all. But, then my professors would lecture, and I would read grammar book after grammar book, and, unfortunately, a lot of the content went over my head. This is why I wanted to write this book. The rules of grammar are very simple once you truly understand them. As writers, I believe that it is our responsibility to perfect our craft every single day, and we can do that by skilling up. I spent hours ensuring that everything in this book makes sense from a real-world perspective. My hope is that you will be able to translate what you learn here and apply it to your own writing.

This book is dedicated to anyone who wants to be a dope writer.
Together, we can do anything!

Introduction

The Dope Grammar Guide is designed for writers who need to sharpen their skills in grammar and basic writing. With its relatable tone, our focus on the basics of grammar will help you to become a more confident, effective, and interesting writer.

This book is guided on the essentials of sentence structure, grammar, and punctuation. The topics addressed in this volume include:

- **Basic Grammar Rules**
- **The 8 Parts of Speech**
  - ✓ *The Noun*
  - ✓ *The Pronoun*
  - ✓ *The Adjective*
  - ✓ *The Verb*
  - ✓ *The Adverb*
  - ✓ *The Preposition*
  - ✓ *The Conjunction*
  - ✓ *The Interjection*

As a writer, in order to be taken seriously, you must produce work that is free of serious mistakes in grammar, spelling, and punctuation. Even before you begin your writing career, strong English skills are crucial. If you are in school, almost every class that you will take requires writing of some kind. You will be expected to write exams, reports, essays, and term papers that are well organized and follow the principles of standard written English. Although, there is a lot more wiggle room, the same rules apply to fiction and non-fiction writers as well. This doesn't mean that you have to be stuffy or hide your amazing personality. Do what works for you but know why you're doing it.

When you learn to recognize the parts of speech, you will be on your way to understanding how the English language works, and you can talk about it intelligently. Even more important, you will be able to identify the tools that will help you to write clear, interesting, and correct sentences as you continue on your path to becoming a dope writer.

Preparing to Write – Checklist

Ask yourself these questions before you get started. By the end of this book, you will be on your way to turning your writing weaknesses into strengths!

1. Do you find yourself in situations in which writing is important?

2. What rituals do you follow before you write? Do you like to have music on? Drink coffee/wine? Do you sharpen your pencil, have to have a certain pen, clean your room, or go on social media?

3. Good writers read! What do you read regularly? (For me, it's the *Shade Room*. Ha! You know I have to get that tea, hunny.) Who are your favorite authors?

4. What are your strengths as a writer?

5. What are your weaknesses as a writer?

6. What makes you dope?

Basic Grammar Rules

For those who just need a quick refresher, you can use this section as a cheat sheet. We will get into some of these topics later in the book.

I.   Spelling Errors

There is no good excuse for spelling errors in a final draft. Everyone should use a dictionary, thesaurus, or turn on Spell Check. Remember, when in doubt, check it out!

II.   Run-on Sentences

Run-ons occur when you try to make one sentence do too much. For example:

✓ *Reagan gazed across the ocean her heart was filled with confusion.*

III.   Avoid run-ons by:

1. Breaking the long sentence into separate sentences:

   ✓ *Reagan gazed across the ocean. Her heart was filled with confusion.*

2. Reducing one of the clauses to a subordinate clause and adding a comma:

   ✓ *When Reagan gazed across the ocean, her heart was filled with confusion.*

3. Adding a comma and coordinating conjunction between the two clauses:

✓ *Reagan gazed across the ocean, but her heart was filled with confusion.*

IV. Sentence Fragments

1. Fragments occur when you've only written part of a sentence. For example:

    ✓ *Because there was no other way escaping the fire.*

2. Fix fragments by making sure your sentence contains *both* a **subject** and a **verb**:

    ✓ *He **(subject)** leaped **(verb)** out of the window because there was no other way of escaping the fire.*

V. Subject/Verb Agreement

1. If the **subject** is *singular*, use a ***singular verb***; if the **subject** is *plural*, use a ***plural verb***:

    ✓ *When my best friend comes through, I **(singular subject)** know **(singular verb)** it's going to be it.*

    ✓ *Jewel and Brandon **(plural subject)** usually attend **(plural verb)** the meeting.*

2. Remember, the subject of a sentence is never contained within a prepositional phrase.

VI. Pronoun Agreement

1. Almost everyone makes this mistake:

    ✓ *Everyone **(singular pronoun)** should get out their **(plural pronoun antecedent)** books.*

2. A pronoun *must agree* in number with its antecedent (the word to which the pronoun refers).

3. Rewrite the sentence using singular pronouns:

   ✓ *Everyone* **(singular pronoun)** *should take out* his **(singular pronoun antecedent)** *or* her **(singular pronoun antecedent)** *book.*

   ✓ **Singular pronouns** include: *each, either, neither, one, everyone, no one, everybody, nobody, anyone, someone, somebody.*

VII.   Verb Tense

Tense means 'time'. **Verbs** tell us what action is occurring and when it is occurring. Verbs change form to indicate when an action takes place. Your writing should remain in one tense, switching only when necessary to the meaning. To fix tenses, read your draft, looking only for tense agreement.

Each main tense is divided into **simple**, **progressive**, **perfect**, and **perfect progressive tenses**.

	Present	Past	Future
Simple	*Finish*	*Finished*	Will *Finish*
Progressive	Am/Is/Are *Finishing*	Was/ Were *Finishing*	Will Be *Finishing*
Perfect	Have/Has *Finished*	Had *Finished*	Will Have *Finished*

Perfect Progressive	Have/Has Been *Finishing*	Had Been *Finishing*	Will Have Been *Finishing*

VIII. Plural & Possessive

An 's' is put at the end of a word for two reasons: *to make it plural* or *to show possession*.

1. When you add an 's' to make a plural, don't use an apostrophe:

   ✓ **Plurals:** *books, students.*

   ✓ **Possessives:** the *book's* *pages; the student's desk.*

   ✓ **Possessiveness for plural nouns:** *the books' pages; all of the students' desks.*

2. Possessive pronouns don't use apostrophes: *yours, hers, its, ours, theirs.*

IX. Capitalization

1. Remember to capitalize proper names, the personal pronoun 'I', names of cities, states, countries, and important words in titles.

2. Titles that should be underlined (or *italicized*) include books, long poems, plays, magazines, movies, published speeches, TV programs, ships, works of art, long musical works, and CDs.

3. Titles that should be in "quotation marks" are short stories, songs, short poems, articles in magazines or newspapers, essays, episodes of a TV program, and chapter titles in books.

X. **Word Usage**

1. *Frequently confused words:*

- Its/It's
  - ✓ *Its = possessive of 'it'*
  - ✓ *It's = it + is*

- To/Too/Two
  - ✓ *To = toward, as far as*
  - ✓ *Too = also, extremely*
  - ✓ *Two = 2*

- Your/You're
  - ✓ *Your = possessive of 'you'*
  - ✓ *You're = you + are*

- Their/They're/There
  - ✓ *Their = possessive of 'they'*
  - ✓ *They're = they + are*
  - ✓ *There = in the place*

2. *Improper Contractions*

Never use *could of, should of, would of.* Instead, use *could have, should have, would have or could've, should've, would've.*

3. *Negatives*

You should only have *one* negative word per sentence.

- ✓ **Example:** *I can't do that.*

- **Negatives** include: *not, don't, can't, won't, shouldn't, wouldn't, didn't, neither/nor, no, nothing.*

4. *Parallel Structure*

All items in a series need to follow the same structure:

✓ **Incorrect:** *He stopped, listened a moment, then <u>he locked</u> the door.*

✓ **Correct:** *He stopped, listened a moment, then <u>locked</u> the door.*

✓ **Incorrect:** *They were singing, dancing, and <u>looked</u> at each other.*

✓ **Correct:** *They were singing, dancing, and <u>looking</u> at each other.*

XI. Punctuation

1. A question ends with a question mark: [?]

2. A semi-colon [;] is <u>not</u> a comma. It joins two clauses of a compound sentence:

   ✓ *Tony was bored with the programs on TV; he decided to go to the library.*

3. A colon [:] introduces a list of items:

   ✓ *Tamara's school had teams for most sports: track, basketball, football, soccer, swimming, and tennis.*

   • A colon also does the job of directing you to the information following it. Think of it as a flashing arrow.

4. Hyphens [-] are used to link words and parts of words.

5. Quotation marks are used as follows:

✓ *"I want to go to the Oakland Coliseum," she explained, "My favorite team is the Warriors."*

XII. <u>Petty Verb Conjunction</u>

There are several troublesome verbs that aren't ordinary, the ones we call **irregular verbs** because they don't take their different forms in standard ways. Most writers occasionally have problems remembering the basic forms of some of the following irregular verbs:

Verb	Present Tense	Past Tense	Past Participle
Begin	Begin	Began	Have Begun
Bring	Bring	Brought	Have Brought
Choose	Choose	Chose	Have Chosen
Come	Come	Came	Have Come
Do	Do	Did	Have Done
Drink	Drink	Drank	Have Drunk
Drive	Drive	Drove	Have Driven
Eat	Eat	Ate	Have Eaten
Fall	Fall	Fell	Have Fallen
Fly	Fly	Flew	Have Flown
Forget	Forget	Forgot	Have Forgotten
Give	Give	Gave	Have Given
Know	Know	Knew	Have Known
Lie	Lie	Lay	Have Lain
Ride	Ride	Rode	Have Ridden
Ring	Ring	Ran	Have Rung
Rise	Rise	Rose	Have Risen
Run	Run	Ran	Have Run
Seek	Seek	Sought	Have Sought
See	See	Saw	Have Seen
Sink	Sink	Sank	Have Sunk
Speak	Speak	Spoke	Have Spoken
Swim	Swim	Swam	Have Swum
Take	Take	Took	Have Taken
Throw	Throw	Threw	Have Thrown
Write	Write	Wrote	Have Written

CHAPTER ONE/THE NOUN.

What is a noun?
a person, place, thing, or idea.

I t's only right to start off with the noun because every English sentence either *contains* one or *is about* one. Nouns can function as subjects, direct objects, indirect objects, objects of a preposition, and **complements**, but we'll get into all that next time.

THE BREAKDOWN:

Nouns have different classes:

- Proper
- Common
- Concrete
- Abstract
- Count
- Non-Count
- Collective

Proper and Common Nouns

Proper nouns name specific, one-of-a-kind things while **common nouns** identify the basic varieties. Proper nouns always begin with a capital letter while common nouns only need capitalization if they start the sentence or are part of a title.

✓ *Robyn* took *Reagan* to the club.

- Robyn, Reagan = **proper nouns**

✓ A _girl_ and her _friend_ went out.

- Girl, friend = **common nouns**

Concrete and Abstract Nouns

You can classify **concrete** and **abstract nouns** by the ability to affect your five senses. If you can see, hear, smell, taste, of even feel the item, it's a concrete noun. If you cannot experience the item with any of your senses, it's abstract.

✓ _Chocolate chip pancakes_ are Reagan's favorite food.

- Chocolate chip pancakes = **concrete noun**
- The subject can see, smell, feel, and but, more importantly, taste the item.

✓ _Bossy never helps clean up after dinner; politeness is not one of her strong points._

- Politeness = **abstract noun**
- You can't see _politeness_, hear, smell, taste, or touch the quality itself.

Count Nouns (Count and Non-Count)

Many nouns can be _singular_ or _plural_; these are **count nouns**.

✓ _Reagan ate three chocolate chip pancakes and four slices of turkey bacon for breakfast._

✓ _Chocolate chip pancakes, slices of bacon_ = **count nouns**

✓ *After over indulging, Reagan got extremely <u>tired</u>.*

    ✓ *Tired* = **non-count noun**
    ✓ You cannot count *tired*.

Collective Noun

Collective nouns have groups. Even though, the group is a single unit, it has more than one member. Some examples are: *army, audience, board, cabinet, class, clique, committee, company, corporation, council, department, faculty, family, firm, gang, group, jury, majority, navy, public, school, society, squad, team, and troop.*

Collective nouns are especially tricky when you are trying to make **verbs** and **pronouns** agree with them. The reason being that collective nouns can be *singular* or *plural*, depending on how the members of the group act.

For example, if the members are acting as a unit— everyone doing the *same thing* at the *same time*, then the **collective noun** is *singular* and requires *singular* **verbs** and **pronouns**.

    ✓ *Despite the danger to <u>itself,</u> <u>the SWAT team pursued</u> Kisino Brown inside the house.*

        ✓ In this sentence, the members of the **collective noun** *team* are going in unison; each officer is engaged in the same activity at the same time, so 'it' as a *singular* **pronoun** and 'pursues', a *singular* **verb**, are necessary.

    ✓ *After <u>they</u> lay out Kisino and his men, the <u>team take off</u> <u>their</u> gear and head to the hospital.*

        ✓ Here, the team members are acting individually. They are not taking off their

3

gear at the same time, so they are not in unison. Instead, each member is undressing as he or she wishes. In cases like this, the **collective noun** is *plural* and requires *plural* **pronouns** like 'their' and *plural* **verbs** like 'take off'.

Keep in mind that a single noun can fall into more than one class.

How to Spot a Noun!

If a word is a noun:

1. It can directly follow articles (*a, an, the*) or quantity words (*some, a lot, ten*).

   ✓ Nouns usually use an article, but not always.

2. It can be made into a *plural* **noun**.

   ✓ Is the word <u>meeting</u> a noun?
      ▪ *'Meeting'* can directly follow articles (*a* and *the*) or quantity words (*some, a lot, ten*):

      ✓ <u>The</u> meeting was held on Thursday.

      ✓ Jewel, Brandon, and Sacario always have to go to <u>a lot</u> of meetings.

Now, you try! If the answer to these two questions is 'yes', then your word is a **noun**.

Practice Quiz

*Part 1: Circle the answer that identifies the **noun** in the sentence:*

1. He will take all of your energy.

    A. Take
    B. All
    C. Your
    D. Energy

2. Jewel was exceedingly proud of his home.

    A. Exceedingly
    B. Home
    C. Proud
    D. Beautiful

3. The San Francisco-Oakland Bay Bridge was built in 1933.

    A. Bridge
    B. Was
    C. Opened
    D. In

4. I can't find my keys.

    A. I
    B. Find
    C. My
    D. Keys

5. When does the party start?

    A. Start
    B. When
    C. Does

        D. Party

6. Stephanie, have you met your new boss?

        A. Have
        B. Met
        C. Your
        D. Boss

7. Reagan tried living in the City, but she couldn't adapt to the cold.

        A. City
        B. But
        C. Couldn't
        D. Adapt

8. Mastering basic grammar is an important goal for writers.

        A. Mastering
        B. Important
        C. Basic
        D. Writers

9. My best friend is coming to visit me tomorrow.

        A. Friend
        B. Coming
        C. Visit
        D. Tomorrow

10. The Bay Area is one of the most interesting places in California.

        A. Most
        B. Interesting
        C. Places
        D. California

For the answers, please go to page 122.

*Part 2: Identify the following nouns as either **Common** or **Proper**. (**Please note**: Words have been purposefully uncapitalized.)*

1. boy _____

2. obama _____

3. california _____

4. son _____

5. uncle mike _____

6. sacramento _____

7. brandon _____

8. house _____

9. bank _____

10. bay area _____

For the answers, please go to page 122.

*Part 3: Write **singular** if the underlined noun is singular or **plural** if it is plural.*

1. _____What <u>schools</u> are the most popular?

2. _____This store has the softest faux <u>furs</u> ever.

3. _____What <u>city</u> has the largest population?

4. _____The <u>capital</u> of California is Sacramento.

5. _____This cell phone weighs less than a deck of <u>cards</u>.

6. _____The houses down the <u>street</u> look like mansions.

7. _____How long have those <u>cars</u> been sitting in the yard?

8. _____Why did they go to that <u>party</u>?

9. _____<u>Students</u> have to study hard if they want to get good grades.

10. _____The <u>mall</u> is fun to walk around in because of all the stores.

For the answers, please go to page 122-123.

CHAPTER TWO/THE PRONOUN.

What is a pronoun?
the words we substitute for nouns.

We would not be anywhere without nouns, but occasionally, in order to avoid repetition, we use other words in place of them.

✓ *As Tony began to take Tony's biology exam, Tony tried to ignore the beeping sound coming from a cellphone behind Tony.*

This sentence is obviously monotonous because of its overuse of *Tony*. We can improve it by using pronouns.

✓ As Tony to take *his* biology exam, *he* tried to ignore the beeping sound coming from a cellphone behind *him*.

The pronouns in this sentence are *his*, *he*, and *him*, and their **antecedent**. The word to which they refer is *Tony.*

THE BREAKDOWN:

Unlike a noun, a **pronoun** does not name a specific person, place, thing, or idea. One probable reason for confusion over pronouns is the existence of so many classes and forms to choose from. Unlike prepositions, conjunctions, and most other parts of speech, pronouns can change their forms or spelling depending on the way they are used in particular sentences. To use them with confidence, it's helpful to recognize the various kinds of pronouns to learn the specific way each kind is used in sentences.

Common Pronouns

I, me, my, mine	we, us, our, ours
you, your, yours	they, them, their, theirs
he, him, his	anybody, everybody, somebody
she, her, hers	everyone, no one, someone
it, its	something, some, all, many, any
who, whose,	each, none, one, this, that, these,
whom	those, which, what

Classes of Pronouns

> I, me, my, mine, he, his, she, her, hers, it, its, we, us, they, them, you, your, yours, our, ours, their, theirs

Pronouns can be classified according to their *form* (the way they are spelled) and their *function* (the way they are used in a sentence):

Personal Pronouns

> I, you, she, he, it, who, whoever, we, they

These pronouns refer to specific individuals, and they are the pronouns most frequently used in writing. **Personal pronouns** can be *singular* or *plural*, and they can be classified by *gender* (masculine, feminine, or neutral) and by *case* (subjective, possessive, and objective), depending on function.

Subjective Pronouns

Subject: *the person, place, thing, or idea that is doing or being something.*

✓ Tony and *I* (not *me)* can explain the equation to you.

✓ Either *he* or *I* (not *her* or *me)* can explain the equation to you.

In some sentences, a pronoun will be the *subject* of an implied verb. This occurs often in comparisons introduced by *than* or *as.* In this situation, the subject form of the pronoun should be used. In the following sentences, the implied verbs are in parentheses.

Predicate Pronouns

A pronoun that comes after some form of the verb *to be* and describes or becomes the *subject* is called a **predicate noun.** It must be a subject pronoun.

✓ That is *she* (not *her*) in the front row. (*She* is a predicate pronoun because it follows the linking verb *is* and renames the subject *that.)*

✓ The last ones to cross the finish line were Prince and *I* (not *me). (I* follows the linking verb *were, so* the subject form *I* is needed.)

✓ Everyone knew that it was *they*. (As in the two sentences above, the pronoun following the linking verb *was* identifies the subject and is in the subject form.)

Now, don't get me wrong. Some exceptions to this rule are allowed. *It is me, It is her,* and *It is them,* for example, are widely used and accepted in casual situations. In conventional speaking and writing though, you should be using *It is I, It is she,* and *It is they.*

Using Subject Pronouns

1. Memorize the **subject pronouns**: *I, you, he, she, it, who, whoever, we,* and *they.*

2. Remember, only subject pronouns can be subjects of verbs.

Objective Pronouns

As their name suggests, **object pronouns** are used as *objects, objects of prepositions, objects of verbs,* and *indirect objects.*

me, you, him, her, it, us, whom, them

Object of a Preposition

A *preposition* is followed by a noun or pronoun. The noun or pronoun is called the **object of the preposition.** When the *object of a preposition* is a pronoun, it must be an **object pronoun.**

✓ Between *you* and *me* (not *I*), her singing is offkey.

✓ Her proud parents stood next to *her* (not *she*) at the capping ceremony.

✓ Solar energy is a possible answer to the energy problems faced by *us* (not *we*) Americans.

When the object of a preposition is a noun or pronoun, there is a mistaken tendency to use the *subject* for the pronoun as in the following sentence:

✓ **Nonstandard:** Smackz's parents gave their concert tickets to Smackz and _I_. (_I_ is the nonstandard form because it is a *subject pronoun*; after a *preposition*, an **object pronoun** should be used.)

The best way to correct sentences like this is to break them up into separate sentences:

✓ **Standard:**

- Tamara surprised Snake with her answer.

- Tamara surprised _me_ (not _I_) with her answer.

- Tamara surprised Snake and _me_ with her answer.

In some sentences, a pronoun will be the *object* of an implied verb. This occurs frequently in comparisons introduced by 'than' and 'as', so the object form of the pronoun should be used. In the following sentences, the implied subjects and verbs are in parentheses:

✓ Ahmad knows my brother much better than (he knows) _me._

✓ The nurse said the shot would hurt her as much as (it hurt) _him._

Using the correct pronoun after 'than' and 'as' is important. What is the difference in meaning between these sentences?

1. My girlfriend likes pizza more than _I_ (do).
2. My girlfriend likes pizza more than (she likes) _me._

Indirect Objects

An **indirect object** is the person or thing to whom or for whom something is done. The indirect object may be thought of as the recipient of the direct object, and it almost always comes between the action verb and the indirect object. When a pronoun is used as an indirect object, the object form of the pronoun should be used.

- ✓ The mail carrier gave _me_ (not _I_) a registered letter.

- ✓ The dealer offered Jewel and _her_ (not _she_) a discount on the tires.

- ✓ Our neighbors sent _us_ (not _we_) a postcard from Barbados.

Using Object Pronouns

1. Memorize the **object pronouns**: _me, you, him, her, it, whom, whomever, us,_ and _them._

2. Use object pronouns when they follow action verbs and prepositions.

Possessive Pronouns

Possessive pronouns are used to show ownerships or possession of one person or thing by another. Most pronouns have two possessive forms.

> _my, mine, our, ours, his, her, hers, its, their, theirs, your, yours_

Use _mine, yours, his, hers, its, ours_ or _theirs_ when the possessive pronoun is separated from the noun that it refers to:

- ✓ The decision was _mine._

✓ The problem became *theirs.*
✓ The car keys that were found were *hers.*

Use *my, your, his, her, its, our,* or *their* when the possessive pronoun comes immediately before the noun it modifies:

✓ It was *my* decision.
✓ It became *their* problem.
✓ She lost *her* car keys.

The *possessive form* is usually used immediately before a noun ending in *-ing.* (Such nouns are called **gerunds**, and they are formed by adding *-ing* words to verbs: *walking, riding, talking, thinking, etc.*

✓ The team objected to *his* taking credit for the job.

✓ *Our* bombing of the harbor was protested by the Cuban delegation.

The possessive forms of *it, who,* and *you* (*its, whose,* and *yours*) cause problems for many writers. Remember that the apostrophe in *it's, who's,* and *you're* indicates that these words are *contractions,* not possessive forms.

Using Possessive Pronouns

Possessive pronouns do not contain apostrophes.

✓ *It's* means *"it is"* or *"it has"* (*Its* is the possessive form).

✓ *Who's* means *"who is"* or *"who has"* (*Whose* is the possessive form).

✓ *You're* means *"you are"* (*Your* is the possessive form).

Indefinite Pronouns

> *all, another, any, anybody, anyone, anything, both, each, either, everybody, everyone, everything, few, many, more, most, much, neither, nobody, none, no one, nothing, one, other, several, some, somebody, someone, something, such*

Although, they function as nouns, **indefinite pronouns** (such as *anyone, someone,* and *somebody)* do not refer to specific individuals.

Demonstrative Pronouns

> *this, that, these, those*

Demonstrative pronouns point out persons or things:

✓ *This* is the house I was born in. *Those* are the trees my father planted.

Demonstrative pronouns are used as adjectives and must agree in number with the nouns they modify. Do not say or write, "these kind," "these sort," "those kind," "those type," and so on.

✓ ***Nonstandard:*** *These kind* of *trees* are common throughout the south.

✓ ***Standard:*** *This kind* of *tree* is common throughout the south.

✓ ***Nonstandard:*** *These type* of *car* always need repairs.

✓ ***Standard:*** This type of car always needs repairs.

Relative Pronouns

who, whose, whom, which, what, that

These pronouns connect or relate groups of words to nouns or other pronouns:

✓ An Iraq veteran suffering from cancer testified *that* it was caused by chemicals used during the war.

As connecting words:

✓ Famine is one of the major problems *that* Africa faces.

Intensive and Reflexive Pronouns

myself, yourself, himself, herself, itself, ourselves, yourselves, themselves

Pronouns ending in *-self* and *-selves.* **Intensive pronouns** stress or emphasize another *noun* or *pronoun.*

✓ I did it *myself.*
✓ You *yourself* are guilty.
✓ She tuned the engine *herself.*
✓ You *yourself* are to blame.

These pronouns should not be used in place of a *subject* or *object pronoun.*

✓ ***Nonstandard:*** My wife and *myself* would be happy to accept your invitation.

✓ ***Standard:*** My wife and *I* would be happy to accept your invitation.

✓ **Nonstandard:** On behalf of my family and *myself*, I would like to express our gratitude to all of you.

✓ **Standard:** On behalf of my family and *me*, I would like to express our gratitude to all of you.

✓ **Nonstandard:** Kevin helped Linda and *myself* install a new transmission in my Chevy.

✓ **Standard:** Kevin helped Linda and *me* install a new transmission in my Chevy.

Reflexive pronouns are used when the action of the sentence is done by the subject to himself or herself.

✓ He helped *himself* to the car.
✓ They let *themselves* into the apartment.
✓ They helped *themselves* to the cookies.
✓ I tried to bathe *myself*.

Using Intensive and Reflexive Pronouns

1. Do not use pronouns ending in *-self* or *-selves* as your subject or object.

2. Never use *hisself, theirself, theirselves,* or *ourself*.

✓ These are nonstandard in both casual and conventional speech and writing, and they should always be avoided.

Interrogative Pronouns

who, whose, whom, which, what

These pronouns introduce questions.

19

✓ *Who* can identify E.J. Cole?
✓ *Whose* phone is this?
✓ *What* is the anticipated population of the US in 2025?

Some Problems with Pronouns: Who and Whom

Not observing the difference between *who* and *whom* is a trap in which some writers sometimes fall. *Whom* has nearly disappeared from casual English. In conventional English, however, the difference between the two words are still very important and should be learned.

The first step to take when selecting the correct form is to determine which word is the *subject* and which is the *object*.

'*Who*' is the **subject** form:

✓ *Who* wants to help me wash the car? (*Who* is the subject of *wants.*)

✓ *Who* do you think wants to help me wash the car? (*Who* is still the subject of *wants* and is not affected by the words that separate it from the verb.)

'*Whom*' is the **object** form:

✓ *Whom* did you see?

✓ With *whom* did you study? (*Whom* is the object of the preposition *with.*)

If you are uncertain about the correct form, substitute with a **personal pronoun** (*she, he, her, him, they, them*). If *he, she,* or *they* fits, use '*who*'; if *her, him,* or *them* fits, use '*whom*'.

✓ I don't know (*who, whom*) he wanted.

- Substitute *him:* He wanted *him.*
  - ✓ The correct form is: I don't know *whom* he wanted.

- ✓ (*Who, Whom*) shall I say is calling?

  - Substitute *she*: *She* is calling.
    - ✓ The correct form is: *Who* shall I say is calling?

Pronoun Agreement

Another area of usage that causes confusion is **pronoun agreement** and reference. Pronouns should agree with the words to which they refer. In other words, if a pronoun refers to a *plural antecedent*, then the pronoun should be *plural.* If the antecedent is singular, then the pronoun should be *singular,* and if the antecedent is a pronoun in the *third person*, then the pronoun should be in third person.

THE BREAKDOWN:

The rules for **pronoun agreement** and reference are usually easy to follow, but there are a few situations in which the choice of a pronoun is *not* always clear or when the antecedent is not obvious. This can result in confusion or ambiguity on the part of the reader as well as the writer. Pronoun agreement and reference are necessary if you want your writing to make sense and be effective.

Agreement in Number

A pronoun must be in agreement in number with its antecedent. If the antecedent is *singular,* then the pronoun is singular. If the antecedent is *plural,* the pronoun is plural. This rule poses no problems in sentences in which the pronouns and antecedents are close as in the following examples:

✓ *Reagan* wanted to buy a *car*, but *she* didn't want to pay more than $9,000 for *it*. (The sentence has two **singular pronouns**, each matched with its **singular antecedent**: *She* (Reagan) and *it* (car).)

✓ Her *parents* told Reagan *they* would be willing to lend her an additional $2,000. (The **plural pronoun** *they* matches its **plural antecedent** *parents*. Do you see another pronoun in this sentence? What is its antecedent?)

✓ *Antoinette* purchased *her* tickets yesterday for the Migos concert. (The singular pronoun *her* matches its singular antecedent *Antoinette*.)

Problems in pronoun agreement occur when the writer loses sight of the antecedent or confuses it with other nouns in the sentence.

✓ **Nonstandard:** The faculty *committee* presented *their* recommendations for new graduation requirements to the deans of the college.

The sentence above is nonstandard because the plural pronoun 'their' does not agree with its singular antecedent 'committee'. How many committees were there? Only one. So, the pronoun referring to it should be singular: *its.*

✓ **Standard:** The faculty *committee* presented *its* recommendations for new graduation requirements to the deans of the college.

In general, use a singular pronoun when the antecedent refers to a specific person or thing.

Some **indefinite pronouns** present exceptions to this general rule—they are always plural, or they can be singular or plural depending on the kind of noun they represent.

The following indefinite pronouns are always singular, which means that the other pronouns referring to them should also be singular: *another, anybody, anyone, anything, each, each one, either, every, everybody, everyone, everything, many a, much, neither, nobody, no one, nothing, one, other, somebody, someone,* and *something.*

Notice that in the following sentences, the indefinite pronouns are accompanied by singular pronouns.

✓ *Anyone* planning a trip to Brazil should apply for a visa before *he* leaves.

✓ *Each* of the girls told me *her* name.

✓ When I returned, *everything* was in *its* place.

✓ *Everyone* was asked to contribute as much as *she* could.

✓ *Everyone* is responsible for making *his* own bed.

✓ *Neither* of the girls wanted *her* picture taken.

You probably noticed the use of masculine pronouns (*he* and *his*) in the first, fourth, and sixth examples. Many people take issue with the exclusive use of masculine pronouns with indefinite pronouns such as *anybody, everyone, someone,* and *everybody.*

The following indefinite pronouns are always plural: *both, a few, many, others,* and *several.* When they are used as antecedents, pronouns referring to them are always plural.

✓ *Many* of his customers transferred *their* accounts to another company.
✓ *A few* of the students admitted *they* had not studied.

✓ *Several* of the golfers said *they* wanted to bring *their* own caddies.

✓ *Both* of the cars had *their* mufflers replaced.

The following indefinite pronouns can be either singular or plural: *all, any, more, most, none,* and *some.*

Antecedents referring to them will be either singular or plural, depending on their meaning and the noun they represent. Antecedents joined by *and* usually take plural nouns.

✓ *Prince Charles and Prince Edward* of England are more famous for *their* private lives than for *their* political views.

✓ *West Germany and East Germany* voted to unite *their* peoples in 1990.

When the antecedents are joined by *and* but refer to a single person or thing, the pronoun may be singular.

✓ *The physicist and Nobel Prize winner* was able to present *her* ideas in terms that students could understand.

✓ *The largest tree and oldest living thing on earth,* the sequoiadendron gigantum is better known by *its* familiar name, the Giant Sequoia.

When the compound antecedent is preceded by 'each' or 'every', a singular pronoun should be used.

✓ *Each* team player and substitute received a certificate recognizing *her* participation.

✓ *Every* father and son was assigned to *his* table.

When two or more antecedents are joined by 'or' or 'nor', the pronouns should agree with the nearer antecedent.

✓ *Neither* the defendant *nor* the witnesses changed *their* testimony.

✓ *Either* the roofers *or* the carpenters left *their* radio in our driveway.

Agreement in Person

If the pronoun agreement breaks down, the reader is distracted and confused. **Agreement in person** is equally important. **Person** refers to the difference among the person speaking *(first person)*, the person spoken to *(second person)*, and the person or thing spoken about *(third person)*.

Pronoun by Person

First-Person: *I, me, my, mine, we, us, our, ours*

Second-Person: *you, your, yours*

Third-Person: *he, him, his, she, her, hers, it, its, they, them, their, theirs*

When you make a mistaken shift in person, you have shown that you have lost your way in your own sentence, that you have forgotten what you were writing about. Here are some examples of confusing shifts in person.

✓ **Shift:** *Swimmers* in the ocean should be very careful because *you* can get caught in rip currents. (This sentence shifts from third-person *swimmers* to second-person *you*.)

✓ **Revised:** *Swimmers* in the ocean should be very careful because *they* can get caught in rip currents.

✓ **Shift:** When *you* fly to St. Louis, *passengers* can see the arch on the bank of the Mississippi River from miles away. (This sentence shifts from second-person _you_ to third-person _passengers_.)

✓ **Revised:** When _you_ fly to St. Louis, _you_ can see the arch on the bank of the Mississippi River from miles away.

✓ **Shift:** When _I_ entered the room, _you_ could smell fresh paint.

✓ **Revised:** When _I_ entered the room, _I_ could smell fresh paint.

The best way to avoid such shifts is to decide in advance who you are talking about and stick to that point of view.

Pronoun Agreement

Pronouns should agree in number with the nouns for which they stand.

1. Determine which noun is the real antecedent.

2. Determine whether the antecedent is _singular_ or _plural_ in meaning.

3. Remember that _singular pronouns_ must refer to _singular antecedents_ and _plural pronouns_ must refer to _plural antecedents._

Pronoun Reference

Pronouns depend on other words—their antecedents—for their meaning. If a **pronoun reference**, the relationship of pronouns to their antecedents, is unclear, its meaning or identity will be confusing. For this reason, you should make certain that every pronoun in your writing (except for indefinite pronouns like _anyone_ and _somebody_) refers specifically to something previously named—its antecedent. In doing so, you will avoid the two most common kinds of problems with pronoun reference: *vagueness* because the writer did not provide a specific antecedent and *ambiguity* because the writer supplied too many antecedents.

Here is an example of each kind of error:

- ✓ **Vague:** Several minor political parties nominate presidential candidates every four years. This is one of the characteristics of the American political system. (What is one of the characteristics of the American political system?)

- ✓ **Ambiguous:** Jacob Hoye wrote a biography of Tupac Shakur that demonstrates his knowledge and sensitivity. (Who demonstrates his knowledge and sensitivity: Jacob Hoye or Tupac?)

By following the accompanying suggestions, you can make clear the relationship between pronouns and their antecedents.

1. The antecedent of a pronoun should be specific rather than implied. Avoid using *that, this, which*, and *it* to refer to implied ideas unless the reference is absolutely clear.

    - ✓ **Vague:** Keisha was so impressed by the lecture given by the astronomer that she decided to major in _it_. (Major in what? _It_ has no antecedent in this sentence.)

    - ✓ **Revised:** Keisha was so impressed by the lecture given by the astronomer that she decided to major in _astronomy_.

    - ✓ **Vague:** Brittany consumes huge quantities of potatoes, spaghetti, and ice cream every day, and *it* is beginning to show. (What is beginning to show?)

✓ **Revised:** Brittany consumes huge quantities of potatoes, spaghetti, and ice cream every day, and *the increase in her weight* is beginning to show.

✓ **Vague:** Athena enjoys singing with music groups at school, and she would like to be a *professional* one day. (A *professional* what?)

✓ **Revised:** Athena enjoys singing with music groups at school, and she would like to be a *professional singer* one day.

Such vague sentences are corrected simply by supplying the missing antecedent.

2. Some sentences are confusing because they have more than one possible antecedent, and the result is ambiguity. To avoid ambiguity, place pronouns as close as possible to their antecedents. Revise sentences in which there are two possible antecedents for one pronoun.

   ✓ **Confusing:** Josh's new car has leather seats, a sunroof, a digital dash with graphic readouts, a vocal warning system, power windows, and an eight-speaker stereo. *It's* power-driven. (What does *it* refer to? What's power-driven?)

   ✓ **Revised:** Jake's new car has leather seats, a sunroof that's power-driven, a digital dash with graphic readouts, a vocal warning system, power windows, and an eight-speaker stereo.

   ✓ **Confusing:** Spanish cooking and Mexican cooking should not be confused; *it* is not as spicy. (What is not as spicy?)

✓ **Revised:** Spanish cooking is not as spicy as Mexican cooking.

Pronoun Reference

1. Don't shift pronouns unnecessarily from one person to another.

2. Learn the pronouns for *first, second,* and *third* person.

3. Make sure that every *that, this, which,* and *it* in your sentences has a clear antecedent.

4. Place pronouns as close as possible to their antecedents.

Avoiding Sexism in Pronoun Usage

One of the movements taking place in our society is the recognition that American English has a masculine bias in almost everything but especially in its use of pronouns. Because English lacks a singular pronoun that refers to both sexes, *he, his,* and *him* have traditionally been used to refer to both men and women when the gender of the antecedent is composed of both males and females or is unknown.

When we constantly use masculine pronouns to personify "the professor," "the lawyer," and "the supervisor," for example, we are subtly rejecting the notion of a female professor, lawyer, and supervisor. Using *he, his,* and *him* as generic terms misleads your audience because those pronouns do not always accurately represent the people behind them.

✓ **Traditional:** A writer can often get ideas when <u>he</u> is listening to music.

Fortunately, there are several ways to make our language gender-fair to avoid the exclusion of our queens. Here's how:

1. **Reword the sentence.**

   ✓ A writer can often get ideas when listening to music.

2. **Change the sentence to the plural form.**

   ✓ Writers often get ideas when _they_ are listening to music.

3. **Substitute another pronoun for the masculine pronoun.**

   ✓ A writer can often get ideas when _she_ is listening to music.

   ✓ A writer can often get ideas when _he_ or _she_ is listening to music.

   ✓ When writing, _one_ can often get ideas while listening to music.

The exclusive use of masculine pronouns (_he, his,_ and _him_) with indefinite pronouns such as _anybody, everyone, someone,_ and _everybody_ is another example of usage that is not gender-fair.

   ✓ **_Traditional:_** Everyone took _his_ seat.

The use of '_his_' in this example to refer to people, in general, is still very common. To avoid the sole use of masculine pronouns, you have three options.

1. **Substitute '_his or her_' for '_his_'.**

   ✓ Everyone took _his or her_ seat.

- Because this form can be awkward, many writers prefer other solutions to this problem.

2. ***Reword the sentence.***

   ✓ The members of the audience took *their* seats.

3. Some writers prefer the following method to avoid only masculine pronouns:

   ✓ Everyone took *their* seats.

While avoiding the exclusive use of the masculine pronouns, the sentence combines a plural pronoun (*their*) with a singular antecedent (*everyone*). Those who prefer this version should be aware that this is not yet accepted as conventional written English.

Practice Quiz

*Part 1: In each of the following sentences, select the appropriate **pronoun** form.*

1. We aren't sure who's driving, but it might be _____ *(her/she)*.

2. Who else could have taken it other than _____ *(he/him)?*

3. Sure, June's tall, but he's not as tall as _____ *(me/I)*.

4. The Chambers and _____ *(they/them)* can't seem to agree on their property lines.

5. The administration wasn't very happy about _____ *(us/our)* stealing the college mascot.

6. We knew that Lanaysia Jackson and _____ *(her/she)* would be great players for Uconn.

7. He didn't think the coach was as smart as _____ *(he/him)*.

8. Except for you and _____ *(I/me)* no one knows about the plot.

9. The judge ordered the landlord and _____ *(she/her)* to rebuild the sidewalk.

10. I can't handle stress as well as _____ *(he/him)*.

For the answers, please go to page 124.

*Part 2: Complete the sentences with appropriate **relative pronouns**.*

1. Maurice had had enough of school, _____ is why he decided to join the Navy.

   A. that
   B. what
   C. whom
   D. where
   E. which

2. If you are planning to drive a long distance, you should drive during the time of the day _____ you are normally awake.

   A. which
   B. whom
   C. when
   D. whose
   E. who

3. In areas _____ many elderly people live alone, the police may visit their homes to make sure they are all right.

   A. that
   B. which
   C. whose
   D. whom
   E. where

4. Canada is one of the few forested nations _____ forests are mostly public property.

A. which
B. that
C. whom
D. whose
E. who

5. In 1851, _____ an international tournament was organized by the great English player Howard Staunton, the modern competitive age of chess began in London.

    A. that
    B. when
    C. which
    D. where
    E. whose

6. I have always found that it's helpful to have a few wise and trusted people to _____ you can turn to for information and advice.

    A. whom
    B. that
    C. whose
    D. who
    E. which

7. While starting your own business the first principle is to select people _____ you have trust and confidence.

    A. on which
    B. whose
    C. in whom
    D. where
    E. of which

8. Jack London, _____ works deal romantically with the overwhelming power of nature and the struggle for survival, was a prolific American novelist and short story writer.

   A. which
   B. whose
   C. where
   D. what
   E. who

9. Parents can learn to create an environment _____ their child can grow and thrive in a more resourceful and less stressful manner.

   A. which
   B. what
   C. where
   D. that
   E. whose

10. Many foods _____ we consume today are all military creations and were first designed for soldiers.

   A. that
   B. of which
   C. where
   D. when
   E. at which

For the answers, please go to page 124

> myself, yourself, himself, herself, itself, ourselves, yourselves, themselves

1. Raheem made this T-shirt _____.

2. Leia did the homework _____.

3. We helped _____ to some lumpia at the party.

4. Ebony, did you take the photo by _____?

5. I wrote this poem _____.

6. He cut _____ with the knife while he was doing the dishes.

7. The lion can defend _____.

8. My mother often talks to _____.

9. Tonya and Gerald, if you want more coconut milk, help _____.

10. Ali and Donte collected the forms _____.

For the answers, please go to page 124.

CHAPTER THREE/THE VERB.

What is a verb?
expresses action or a state of being.

Every sentence that you write contains a verb. Sometimes, the verb is only implied; usually, it's stated though. When you can recognize and use verbs correctly, you have taken a big step toward being a better speaker and writer.

THE BREAKDOWN:

A **verb** tells what a noun or pronoun does or what it is. If the verb tells us what a noun or pronoun does, it is an **action verb.**

- ✓ Rashida *paints* beautiful pictures, which she *hides* in her attic.

- ✓ Hakeem *attends* medical school in L.A.

If the verb expresses a state of being rather than action, it is a **linking verb.** Linking verbs *do not* express action; instead, they connect a noun or pronoun with a word or group of words that describe or rename the subject.

- ✓ The subject of tonight's debate *is* prayers in public school. (*Subject* is linked by the verb *is* to *prayers*, a word that renames it.)

✓ I.Q. tests *are* reliable predictors of academic success, according to many educators. (*Tests* is linked to *predicators* by the verb *are*.)

✓ My new speakers *sound* much better than my old ones. (*Speakers* is linked to the words that describes it—*better*—by the verb *sound*.)

✓ Computers were very expensive for the average family to purchase in the 70s. (What words are linked? What word links them?)

✓ Belize is a small nation in Central America. (What word renames Belize? How are the two words linked?)

The most common linking verbs are formed from the verb *to be: am, are, is, was,* and *were.* Other words often used as linking verbs are *appear, become, grow, remain, seem,* and the "sense" verbs: *feel, look, smell, sound,* and *taste.*

Verbs are the only words that change their spelling to show tense. **Tense** is the time when the action of the verb occurs. Notice in the following sentences how the tense or time of the action is changed by the spelling of the verb.

✓ Our mayor *delivers* an annual message to the citizens of our city. (Present tense)

✓ Last week, he *delivered* his message on local television. (Past tense)

To show additional difference in meaning, verbs often use helping words that suggest the time at which the action of the verb takes place and other kinds of meaning. These words are called **helping/auxiliary verbs**, and they always come before the main verbs. Verbs that consist of helping verbs and a main verb are called **verb phrases**. Look carefully at the following sentences:

- ✓ I _will_ go.
- ✓ He _had_ studied.
- ✓ Zoie _did_ not want lunch.
- ✓ The sisters _were_ saddened.
- ✓ The child _was_ photographed.
- ✓ They might _have been_ selected.

Each of the verbs in the preceding sentences consists of a helping/auxiliary verb and a main verb. Here are the common helping/auxiliary verbs. You should try to memorize them.

Common Helping/Auxiliary Verbs

can, could

may, might, must, ought

shall, should, will, would

have, has, had

do, does, did

am, is, are, was, were, been, be, being

Some verbs can be either helping/auxiliary verbs or main verbs. In other words, if they appear alone without a helping verb/auxiliary verb, they are main verbs. But, if they come before a main verb, they are helping/auxiliary verbs or main verbs.

Forms of _to be_: _am, is, are, was, were_

Forms of _to do_: _do, does, did_

Forms of _to have_: _has, have, had_

Recognizing Verbs

1. An **action verb** is a word that fits in the slot in the following sentence:

"I (or He or She or They) usually_____."

✓ I usually *jog.*
✓ She usually *snores.*
✓ They *were* happy.

2. A **linking verb** is a word that fits in the following sentence:

"I (or He or She or They)_____ happy."

✓ I *am* happy.
✓ He *is* happy.
✓ They *were* happy.

To improve your writing, you should master the sentence and its two main parts—the *subject* and the *verb.* Once you have mastered this skill, you will be on your way to writing more effective sentences.

The Subject and the Verb

The **subject** of a sentence names a person, place, thing, or idea; it tells us *who* or *what* the sentence is about. The **verb** describes action or the subject's state of being; it tells us what the subject *does*, what the subject *is,* or what the subject *receives.*

                    (s)   (v)
✓ Francis Scott Key wrote the words to our national anthem.

    (s)   (v)
✓ <u>Sacramento</u> <u>is</u> the capital of California.

    (s)   (v)
✓ <u>Gertrude Ederle</u> <u>was</u> the first woman to swim the English Channel.

    (s)   (v)
✓ <u>Chance the Rapper</u> <u>received</u> the 2017 BET Humanitarian Award.

  (s)   (v)
✓ <u>I</u> rarely <u>eat</u> this much licorice.

Each of the above sentences contain a subject and a verb, and each makes a complete statement. In other words, they convey a sense of completeness. In a conversation, sentences often lack stated subjects and verbs, but their contexts—the words and sentences that surround them—make the missing subject and verb clear.
For example:

✓ **Terrance:** "Studying your sociology?"
✓ **Noah:** "Yes, big test tomorrow."
✓ **Terrance:** "Ready for it?"
✓ **Noah:** "Hope so. Flunked the last one."

If this conversation were written in conventional sentences, the missing subjects and verbs would be supplied, and the exchange might look like this.

✓ **Terrance:** "Are you studying your sociology?"
✓ **Noah:** "Yes, I have a big test tomorrow."
✓ **Terrance:** "Are you ready for it?"
✓ **Noah:** "I hope so. I flunked the last one."

All sentences have subjects either stated or implied. Before moving on, it is important that you are able to locate the subject and the verb in a sentence. Because it is usually easier to locate, the verb is the best place to start.

Finding the Verb

The verb in a sentence may be a single word (he *sleeps*) or a verb phrase of two, three, or even four words (he *had slept*, he *had been sleeping*, he *must have been sleeping.*)

Action Verbs

Action verbs tell what the subject does.

- ✓ The students *boarded* the plane for San Juan. (What did the students do? They *boarded.* The verb in this sentence is *boarded*.)

- ✓ Visitors to Disneyland *buy* souvenirs for their friends at home. (What do visitors do? They *buy* souvenirs. The verb is *buy*.)

Verbs are either *active* or *passive* in voice. In the active voice, the subject and verb relationship is straightforward: the subject is the doer. In the passive voice, the subject of the sentence is not the doer. It is shown with *by + doer* or is not shown in the sentence. Passive voice is used when the action is the focus, not the subject. It is important (or not known) who does the action.

- ✓ The window is broken. (It is not known who broke the window, or it is not important to know who broke the window.)

- ✓ The class has been cancelled. (The focus is on the class being cancelled. It is not important to know who cancelled it.)

Passive voice should be avoided when you want more clarity in writing, but, in some cases, you need to use passive voice to stress the action, not the actor. Also, passive voice can be considered nicer as it sounds less aggressive or dramatic.

✓ The building was built in 1990.
✓ Your business is appreciated.

You can easily rewrite an active sentence to a passive sentence. The object in the active sentence becomes a subject in the passive sentence. The verb is changed to a *'be' verb + past participle.* The subject of the active sentence followed by *by* is omitted.

✓ *Sam wrote a letter to Jamie.*
✓ *A letter was written to Jamie by Sam.*

✓ *The government built a new bridge.*
✓ *A new bridge was built by the government.*

Linking Verbs

Some verbs do not show action. Instead, they express a condition or state of being. They are called **linking verbs**, and they link the subject to another word that renames or describes the subject.

Most linking verbs are formed from the verb *to be* and include *am, are, is, was,* and *were.* Several other verbs often used as linking verbs are *appear, become, feel, grow, look, remain, seem, smell, sound,* and *taste.*

The verbs in the following sentences are linking verbs. They link their subjects to words that rename or describe them.

✓ My parents *seem* happy in their new apartment. (The linking verb *seem* connects the subject *parents* with the word that describes them: *happy.)*

✓ The first-graders *remained* calm during the earthquake. (The verb *remained* connects the subject _first-graders_ with the words that describes them: _calm._)

When looking for the verb in a sentence, you should remember that it sometimes consists of more than one word. In such cases, it is called a verb phrase, and **verb phrases** consist of a main verb and a helping/auxiliary verb. Any helping/auxiliary verbs in front of the main verb are part of the verb.

- ✓ _may have_ disappeared.
- ✓ _should be_ avoided.
- ✓ _might_ stay.
- ✓ _did_ guarantee.
- ✓ _is_ speaking.
- ✓ _could have_ objected.

Words Mistaken for the Verb

You may sometimes be confused by two forms of the verb that may be mistaken for the main verb of the sentence. These forms are the **infinitive** and **present participle.**

The **infinitive** is the "to" form of the verb: _to leave, to write, to start,_ and so on. The infinitive is the base form of the verb—in other words, it basically names the verb. It does not give us any information about its person, its tense, or its number. **Note:** The infinitive by itself is _never_ the verb of the sentence.

- ✓ My reading comprehension _to improve_ by 15%.

- ✓ Contractors _to build_ cheaper and smaller homes in the future.

These word groups are not sentences because they try to make an infinitive do the work of the main verb. They can be corrected by placing a verb before the infinitive.

- ✓ My reading comprehension _was_ to improve by 15%.

✓ Contractors <u>vow</u> to build cheaper and smaller homes in the future.

Of course, these word groups could also have been converted to sentences simply by changing the infinitives to main verbs: *improved* and *will build*.

The other form of the verb that sometimes looks as though it is the main verb is the **present participle**—the "-ing" form of the verb, such as: *leaving, starting, writing,* etc. Like the infinitive, the present participle can never stand by itself as the verb in a sentence. Notice how the following groups of words fail to make sense because they attempt to use the present participle—the "-ing" form—as their verb.

✓ My reading comprehension <u>improving</u> by 15%.

✓ Contractors <u>building</u> cheaper and smaller homes in the future.

These word groups can be corrected by placing a form of the verb *to be* in front of the present participle.

✓ My reading comprehension <u>has been improving</u> by 15%.

✓ Contractors <u>will be building</u> cheaper and smaller homes in the future.

Something to look out for: you will never find the verb of a sentence in a prepositional phrase. The reason for this rule is simple. **Prepositional phrases** are made up of prepositions and their objects, which are either nouns or pronouns—never verbs. Therefore, a prepositional phrase will never contain the verb of the sentence.

Finding the Verb

1. Find the verb by asking what actions take place.

2. Find the verb by asking what word links the subject to the rest of the sentence.

3. If a word fits in the following slot, it is a verb:

   "I (or He or She or They) _____."

   ✓ I *hunt* Elk.
   ✓ She *swims* every morning.
   ✓ They *bring* us flowers each time they visit.

4. Remember that the verb in a sentence will never have the infinitive (*"to"* form) in front of it.

5. The (*"-ing"*) form (the present participle) can be a verb if it has a helping verb in front of it.

6. The verb will never be in a prepositional phrase.

Common Errors Involving Verbs

One reason why so many mistakes are made in verb usage is that most sentences contain more than one verb, and because of that, there are more chances to go wrong. Furthermore, the verbs most often used in the English language are irregular, which means that they change in a variety of ways. To be on the safe side, they must be memorized.

To make matters even worse, verbs change their forms and appearance more often than any other part of speech. As a result, they force us to pick through them carefully.

Despite the difficulties mentioned above, problems with verbs fall into a few manageable categories. A common one is not knowing the correct form of the verb needed to express when a particular action is taking place. Another difficulty is not knowing the correct form of an irregular verb.

Look at the following sentences to see whether you have been using the correct verb form. Each sentence contains a verb that is often used incorrectly. The incorrect verb is in parentheses.

✓ Lila was thrilled that we _came_ (not _come_ to see her at the hospital.

✓ I slept in and then learned that my friends had _gone_ (not _went_) for coffee without me.

If you discover that you have been using any of these verbs incorrectly, this chapter will give you some dope tips for their correct usage. We will begin by examining the principal parts of regular and irregular verbs and will then move on to the most common problems connected with the use of these verbs, including shifts in tense and troublesome pairs like '_lie_' and '_lay_' and '_sit_' and '_set_'.

All verbs have four principal parts (or forms): the _present,_ the _past,_ the _past participle_, and the _present participle._ By learning these four parts, you can build all the verb tenses. When we talk about the tense of a verb, we mean the time expressed by the verb: the _present, past,_ or _future_ tense.

Regular Verbs

Regular Verbs form the **past** and **past participl**e by adding -ed or -d to their present forms (_watch, watched,_ and _watched_). The past participle is the form used with the helping verbs _have, had,_ or _had_ or with a form of _be_ (**have been watched** and **were watched**). The **present participle** is formed by adding -ing to the **present form**, and it is used with a form of *to be* to form the other tenses (*am studying, was studying, have been studying,* etc.)

Here are the four principle parts of common regular verbs.

Present	Past	Past-Participle	Present-Participle
Shop	Shopped	Shopped	Shopping
Dance	Danced	Danced	Dancing
Wash	Washed	Washed	Washing
Love	Loved	Loved	Loving
Help	Helped	Helped	Helping

Notice that the past (*stopped, danced, washed,* etc.) and the past participle are identical and are formed by adding '*-ed*' or '*-d*' to the present form. The past participle is used with helping verbs to form past tenses: *I have talked, I had talked,* and *she has talked; I was helped, we were helped,* and *they had been helped.*

Irregular Verbs

Irregular Verbs are irregular in the way their past participle forms are made. Instead of adding '*-ed*' or '*-d*' to their past and past participle forms, irregular verbs change in ways that cannot be predicted. This means that you will have to memorize their past and past participle forms. Fortunately, irregular verbs form their present participles in the same way as regular verbs: by adding -*ing* to the present form.

To understand why it is difficult to make any generalization about irregular verbs, let us examine the verbs '*sing*' and '*bring*'. From our familiarity with the English language, we know that '*sing*' is the present ("I *sing* in church every Sunday."), '*sang*' is the past ("I *sang* last Sunday."), and *'sung'* is the past participle ("I have *sung* every Sunday this month.").

<u>*Suggestions for Using Irregular Verbs*</u>

1. Resist the temptation to add *-ed* to an irregular verb. Do not write or say *catched, bursted, knowed,* etc.

2. Use *have, has,* and *had* with the past participle forms to form past tenses.

   ✓ She <u>*has*</u> *done* several music videos for her newest album.

   ✓ I <u>*have*</u> *flown* in an airplane and *ridden* on the train.

<u>*Common Irregular Verbs and Problem Regular Verbs*</u>

Present	Past	Past-Participle	Present-Participle
[I] arise	[I] arose	[I have] arisen	[I am] arising
awake	awoke, awakened	awoken	awaking
bear (carry)	bore	borne	bearing
begin	began	began	beginning
blow	blew	blown	blowing
break	broke	broken	breaking
bring	brought	brought	bringing
burst	burst	burst	bursting

catch	caught	caught	catching
choose	chose	chosen	choosing
come	came	come	coming
dig	dug	dug	digging
dive	dived, dove	dived	diving
do	did	done	doing
drag	dragged	dragged	dragging
draw	draw	drawn	drawing
drink	drank	drunk	drinking
drive	drove	driven	driving
drown	drowned	drowned	drowning
eat	ate	eaten	eating
fly	flew	flown	flying
freeze	froze	frozen	freezing
give	gave	given	giving
go	went	gone	going
grow	grew	grown	growing
hang	hung	hung	hanging
hang (execute)	hanged	hanged	hanging
hide	hid	hidden	hiding
know	knew	known	knowing
lay	laid	laid	laying
lead	led	led	leading
leave	left	left	leaving

lie	lay	lain	lying
light	lighted, lit	lighted, lit	lighting
ride	rode	ridden	riding
ring	rang	rung	ringing
rose	rose	risen	rising
run	ran	run	running
see	saw	seen	seeing
set	set	set	setting
shake	shook	shaken	shaking
shine (glow)	shone	shone	shining
shine (polish)	shined	shined	shining
shrink	shrank, shrunk	shrunk, shrunken	shrinking
sing	sang	sung	singing
sink	sank	sunk	sinking
sit	sat	sat	sitting
sleep	slept	slept	sleeping
sneak	sneaked	sneaked	sneaking
speed	sped	sped	speeding
spring	sprang	sprung	springing
strike	struck	struck	striking
swim	swum	swum	swimming
swing	swung	swung	swinging

take	took	taken	taking
tear	tore	torn	tearing
throw	threw	thrown	throwing
wake	woke, waked	waked, woken	walking
wear	wore	worn	wearing
write	wrote	written	writing

Forming the Past Tense, Past Participle, and Present Participle Forms

1. To form the past and past participle forms of a regular verb, add '-ed' or '-d' to the present form. To form the present participle, add '-ing' to the present form.

2. Irregular verbs change their spelling, and therefore have to be memorized. Study the list on (pages 55-58) for the correct past and past participle forms of irregular verbs.

3. Use *am, is, was, were, has been,* and other forms of 'be' with the past participle forms to form all verbs in the passive voice.

   ✓ The dogs _were_ caught before they could attack anyone.

   ✓ Vanya _was_ given a varsity letter for managing the softball team.

4. Use forms of 'be' before the present participle to form tenses where the action continues to happen.

✓ Grammar *is beginning* to make sense to me.

✓ They *have been winning* more of their matches this season.

Use the Correct Tense

The forms of the verb change according to the time expressed—when the action or state of being occurs. Each tense has a specific purpose, and strategic writers select the appropriate tense according to that purpose.

Here is a list of the six common tenses in English and their uses.

Present: I *jog* or I *am jogging.*

Past: I *jogged* or I was *jogging.*

Future: I will *jog* or I will be *jogging.*

Present Perfect: *I have* jogged or I have been *jogging.*

Past Perfect: I had *jogged* or I had been *jogging.*

Future Perfect: I will have *jogged* or I will have been *jogging.*

Each of the six tenses has an additional form called the **progressive form**, which expresses action that continues to happen. The progressive form is not a separate tense but an additional form of each of the six tenses in the conjugation. It consists of a form of the verb '*be*' + the present participle of the verb.

Progressive Forms

Present Progressive: *am, are, is* talking

Past Progressive: *was, were* talking

Future Progressive: *will be* talking

Present Perfect Progressive: *has, have been* talking

Past Perfect Progressive: *had been* talking

Future Perfect Progressive: *will have been* talking

The **present tense** is used in the following situations:

To express a condition or an action that exists or is going on now.

- ✓ Her car *is* fast.

- ✓ But she *is driving* under the speed limit.

To express an action that is habitual or is always true.

- ✓ He always *beats* his opponents.

- ✓ There *is* no game like basketball.

The **past tense** expresses an action or condition completed in the past.

- ✓ Bobby *visited* his mother last night.

- ✓ The coalition forces *attacked* the terrorists in their caves.

The *future tense* expresses an action that will take place in the future.

- ✓ Javier <u>will race</u> his bicycle in the next Olympics.

- ✓ Uncle Mike <u>will be</u> 50-years old in August.

The **present perfect** tense is used for an action that began in the past and continues in the present.

- ✓ I <u>have lived</u> in Hayward since 2011. (And I still live in Hayward.)

The **present perfect** tense can also be used for an action that started in the past and has been completed at some indefinite time.

- ✓ The fire in the warehouse <u>has been extinguished</u>.

- ✓ My grandfather <u>has been</u> to a doctor only once in his life.

The **past perfect** tense is used for an action that began and ended in the past. Additionally, it conveys that the action was completed before something else happened.

- ✓ I <u>had lived</u> in Sacramento before I moved to Hayward. (**Not**: I *lived* in Sacramento before I moved to Hayward.)

- ✓ Monica asked us if we <u>had watched</u> the newest episode of *Love & Hip Hop*. (Not: Monica asked us if we *watched* the newest episode of *Love & Hip Hop*.)

The **future perfect tense** is used for an action that will end in the future before a particular time.

- ✓ Her parents <u>will have been</u> married forty years this Thanksgiving.

✓ I *will have used* up all of my vacation time by the time your visit ends next week.

A Few Suggestions for Using the Correct Tense

1. Do not use the past tense of a verb when it should be in the present tense.

   ✓ Naomi took a course in anthropology last year. She said that it *was* an interesting subject that *studied* culture and societies throughout the world. (Incorrect: *was* and *studied* imply that anthropology no longer is interesting and no longer studies other societies and culture. The correct verbs are *is* and *studies*.)

2. Use the present infinitive (*to write, to invent, to leap,* etc.) unless the action referred to was completed before the time expressed in the governing verb.

   ✓ Annika and Sanjay planned *to stay* (not *to have stayed*) awake for SNL.

   ✓ I am fortunate *to have had* (not *to have*) my husband's jacket during the stormy boat trip.

3. When a narrative in the past tense is interrupted by a reference to a preceding event, use the past perfect tense.
   ✓ No one could believe that I *had known* him before he became a rap star.

   ✓ The film's ending made no sense to me because I *had missed* the beginning.

Reminders: About Tenses

1. Use the past tense only if the action referred to took place at a specific time in the past.

2. Use the past perfect tense (I *had* + the past participle) only when you want to place a completed action before another action in the past.

Shifts in Tense

Having learned the use of the six common tenses, you should use them consistently to avoid unnecessary shifts from one tense to another. If, for example, you begin a paragraph using the past tense to describe events in the past, do not suddenly jump to the present tense to describe those same events. Similarly, don't abruptly shift to the past tense if you are narrating an incident in the present tense. This does not mean that you can't use more than one tense in a piece of writing, but it does mean that you must use the same tense when referring to the same period of time.

Two Pairs of Irregular Verbs: Lie and Lay and Sit and Set

There are four irregular verbs that cause more trouble than most of the others: *lie, lay, sit,* and *set.* Unwary writers can easily confuse them, but dope writers observe their differences.

Lie and Lay

'To lie' means "to remain in position or to be at rest." (For this purpose, we are ignoring the other meaning— "to tell a falsehood".) When *'lie'* carries this meaning, it is a regular verb. *'Lie'* never takes an object, so that means you would never *'lie'* anything down. *'Lie'* is usually followed by a word or phrase that tells where (*lie* down, *lie* on the grass, etc.)

The principal parts of *'lie'* are:

- *lie* (the present)

- *lay* (the past)
- *lain* (the past participle)
- *lying* (the present participle)

Because our ear tells us that a 'd' sound is usually the sign of the past tense, we are tempted to say or write '*laid*' for the past tense instead of the correct form '*lay*'. The present participle '*lying*' is used with helping verbs; it should not be confused with '*laying*'.

Forms of Lie

Present: Our dog often <u>*lies*</u> by the fire on cold nights.

Past: Rob <u>*lay*</u> (not *laid*) by the pool for hours yesterday.

Past Participle: The dishes have <u>*lain*</u> (not *laid*) in the sink all day.

Present Participle: The children have been <u>*lying*</u> (not *laying*) on the porch and telling ghost stories.

'*To lay*' means "to place or put something somewhere," and it is a **transitive verb**. It requires an object to complete its meaning. "Lay the *package* <u>down</u>," "Lay your <u>*head*</u> down," etc.

The principal parts of '*lay*' are:

- *lay* (the present)
- *laid* (the past)
- *laid* (the past participle)
- *laying* (the present participle)

The present participle '*laying*' is used with helping verbs; it is followed by an object.

Forms of Lay

Present: Please *lay* your essay on my desk.

Past: Nathan *laid* his Warriors hat on the floor under his chair.

Past Participle: We have *laid* over 200 bricks in the new driveway.

Present Participle: We were *laying* bricks in uneven lines and had to remove them.

The most effective way of mastering '*lie*' and '*lay*' is to memorize their forms: *lie, lay, lain,* and *lying; lay, laid, laid,* and *laying.*

Sit and Set

'*To sit*' means "to occupy a seat." It is not a **transitive verb**, so it never takes an object. This means that you never "sit" anything down.

The principal parts are:

- *sit* (the present)
- *sat* (the past)
- *sat* (the past participle)
- *sitting* (the present participle)

Forms of Sit

Present: Spike Lee *sits* in the front row at many Knicks games.

Past: We always *sat* in the back row at the movies.

The Dope Grammar Guide

> **Past Participle:** My sister *has sat* next to us in Spanish class all year.
>
> **Present Participle:** Have you been *sitting* in the balcony for all of the performances this season?

'To set' resembles *'to lay'* in meaning. *'To set'* means "to put in place." Like *'to lay'*, it is a transitive verb and is followed by another word (a direct object) to complete its meaning.

Its principal parts remain the same in all forms:

- *set* (the present)
- *set* (the past)
- *set* (the past participle)
- *setting* (the present participle)

Forms of Set

Present: Joey always <u>sets</u> his alarm clock in the morning.

Past: Last night, I <u>set</u> the volume control to high and almost blew my speakers.

Past Participle: I *have* <u>set</u> your Cardi B disc back on the shelf.

Present Participle: <u>Setting</u> his old records near the heater was careless.

Using *Lie* and *Lay* and *Sit* and *Set*

1. *'To lie'* means "to be at rest." You don't "lie" anything down. The forms are *lie, lay, lain*, and *lying*.

2. *'To lay'* means "to place or put somewhere." An object must always follow this verb. The forms are *lay, laid, laid,* and *laying.*

3. *'To sit'* means "to occupy a seat." You don't "sit" anything down. The forms are sit, *sat, sat,* and *sitting.*

4. *'To set'* means "to put in place" and is always followed by an object. The forms do not change in the present, the past, or the past participle: *set, set,* and *set.* The present participle is *setting.*

Practice Quiz

*Part 1: Circle the **subject** and underline the **verb** in each sentence.*

1. We can heavily influence our chances of developing cancer.

2. Unhealthy choices cause most cancer deaths.

3. These include smoking, poor diet and obesity, and lack of exercise.

4. Only a few deaths are caused by other factors.

5. These factors are environmental carcinogens, family history, alcohol, and virus.

6. Simple lifestyle alterations can significantly reduce the risks of developing cancer.

7. First of all, smokers must stop smoking.

8. How can we consume five or more servings of fruits and vegetables daily?

9. Consumption of grains and beans should exceed that of meat and fat in the diet.

10. Finally, exposure to the sun's ultraviolet rays should be avoided.

For the answers, please go to page 125.

Part 2: Choose the sentence that contains the correct **subject-verb agreement**.

1. When Dad comes home, nobody _____ to admit to the spilled red paint on the floor.

    A. want
    B. wants

2. Either one of the boys or their sister _____ the likely culprit.

    A. is
    B. are

3. If somebody _____ red paint on his or her hands, we may have the answer.

    A. has
    B. have

4. Each of the children _____ a slightly different story.

    A. tells
    B. tell

5. Both of the boys _____ their hands are clean.

    A. insists
    B. insist

6. Neither of their paintings _____ done in any red paint.

    A. was
    B. were

7. _____ this give a clue?

    A. Do

B. Does

8. Evidence _____ being carefully considered by Dad as he inspects things.

   A. are
   B. is

9. There _____ three trays of paint: Tiffany blue, lemon yellow, and fire engine red.

   A. is
   B. are

10. The remaining red paint _____ directly in front of Amie.

   A. sit
   B. sits

For the answers, please go to page 125.

Part 3: Choose the sentence in which the underlined irregular verb is used correctly.

1.
  - A. After they came in from school, I <u>sweeped</u> the kitchen floor.
  - B. After they came in from school, I <u>swept</u> the kitchen floor.
  - C. After they came in from school, I <u>sweep</u> the kitchen floor.

2.
  - A. She insisted she'd never have <u>say</u> that.
  - B. She insisted she'd never have <u>said</u> that.
  - C. She insisted she'd never have <u>sayed</u> that.

3.
  - A. At the end of our successful meeting, he <u>shook</u> hands with me.
  - B. At the end of our successful meeting, he <u>shaked</u> hands with me.
  - C. At the end of our successful meeting, he <u>shaken</u> hands with me.

4.
  - A. The seamstress <u>sticked</u> herself with her new scissors.
  - B. The seamstress <u>stuck</u> herself with her new scissors.
  - C. The seamstress <u>stook</u> herself with her new scissors

5.
  - A. The delay wasn't as long as he had <u>thought</u>.
  - B. The delay wasn't as long as he had <u>thinked</u>.
  - C. The delay wasn't as long as he had <u>thunk</u>.

6.
   A. When the boy arrived home, he <u>fed </u>the goat before he did his homework.
   B. When the boy arrived home, he <u>feed</u> the goat before he did his homework.
   C. When the boy arrived home, he <u>feeded</u> the goat before he did his homework.

7.
   A. All last month, he <u>fighted </u>with his brother over the settlement.
   B. All last month, he <u>fought</u> with his brother over the settlement.
   C. All last month, he <u>fit</u> with his brother over the settlement.

8.
   A. Last week, she <u>buy</u> her son a new pair of cleats for baseball.
   B. Last week, she <u>buyed</u> her son a new pair of cleats for baseball.
   C. Last week, she <u>bought</u> her son a new pair of cleats for baseball.

9.
   A. He arrived home and <u>told</u> her about his new plans for the weekend.
   B. He arrived home and <u>tolled</u> her about his new plans for the weekend.
   C. He arrived home and <u>tell</u> her about his new plans for the weekend.

10.
   A. Did he get <u>hurt</u> when he fell from the oak tree?
   B. Did he get <u>hurted</u> when he fell from the oak tree?
   C. Did he get <u>hart</u> when he fell from the oak tree?

For the answers, please go to page 125.

CHAPTER FOUR/THE ADVERB.

What is an adverb?
words that describe or modify verbs,
adjectives, and other adverbs.

Adverbs modify verbs, adjectives, and other adverbs.

✓ The *extremely* *tall* guard *dribbled* the basketball *slowly*. (*Extremely* modifies the adjective *tall*, and *slowly* modifies the verb *dribbled*.)

✓ The tall guard dribbled the basketball *very* slowly. (*Very* modifies the adverb *slowly*.)

THE BREAKDOWN:

Adverbs usually answer the following questions:

* *When?*
* *Where?*
* *How?*
* *To what extent?*

✓ **When:** Hector *immediately* realized that he had confused Michelle with her sister. (The adverb *immediately* modifies the verb *realized*.)

✓ **Where:** Please, wait *here*. (The adverb *here* modifies the verb *wait*.)

✓ **How:** The deer struggled *unsuccessfully* to escape. (The adverb *unsuccessfully* modifies the verb *struggled*.)

✓ **To What Extent:** The state capitol building was _completely_ remodeled. (The adverb _completely_ modifies the verb _was remodeled._)

Adjectives and **adverbs** are often confused, but remember, adjectives describe nouns and pronouns.

✓ Her _loud_ hiccups distracted the speaker. (_Loud_ is an adjective because it modifies _hiccups_.)

✓ If you sneeze _loudly_, you will distract the speaker. (_Loudly_ is an adverb because it modifies the verb _sneeze_.)

Recognizing Adverbs

1. Adverbs are words that will fit in the following slot:

"He will meet us _____."

2. Adverbs tell _when, where, how_, and _to what extent_.

✓ He will meet us _later_. (When)
✓ He will meet us _here_. (Where)
✓ He will meet us punctually. (How)
✓ He will meet us _briefly_. (To what extent)

Many adverbs are formed by adding '–ly' to the adjective, but keep in mind that some adverbs do not end in '-ly'. (_above, near, there, very,_ etc.) On the other hand, some words that end in '-ly' are not adverbs (words such as _silly, friendly,_ and _lovely._) Adverbs modify a verb, an adjective, or another adverb.

Conjunctive Adverbs

Conjunctive adverbs are words that join independent clauses into one sentence. A conjunctive adverb helps you create a shorter sentence.

When you use a conjunctive adverb, put a semicolon (;) before it and a comma (,) after it.

✓ We have many different sizes of this shirt; _however_, it comes in only one color.

Some examples of conjunctive adverbs are _accordingly, also, besides, consequently, finally, however, instead, likewise, meanwhile, moreover, nevertheless, next, otherwise, still, therefore, then._

✓ The baby fell asleep; _then_, the doorbell rang.

✓ The due date for the final paper has passed; _therefore_, I could not submit mine on time.

Conjunctive adverbs look like coordinating conjunctions (_and, but, or, so, for, yet, nor_); however, they are not as strong as coordinating conjunctions, and they are punctuated differently.

A conjunctive adverb is also used in a single main clause. In this case, a comma (,) is used to separate the conjunctive adverb from the sentence.

✓ I woke up very late this morning. _Nevertheless_, I wasn't late for school.

✓ She didn't take the bus to work today. _Instead_, she drove her car.

Adverbs can usually appear in three positions in a sentence. They can appear at the beginning.

✓ _Yesterday_, a rainbow appeared in the western sky.

They can appear in the middle.

    ✓ A rainbow appeared *yesterday* in the western sky.

They can appear at the end.

    ✓ A rainbow appeared in the western sky <u>yesterday</u>.

There are a few situations in which we cannot place adverbs randomly. Do not place adverbs between a verb and its object.

    ✓ Max plays the piano <u>*beautifully*</u>. (**Not**: Max plays *beautifully* the piano.)

    ✓ Laine <u>*often*</u> forgets her new telephone number. (**Not**: Laine forgets *often* her new telephone number.)

Do not place adverbs before *am, is, are, was,* and *were* when the adverbs (*always, never, ever, usually, often, sometimes,* etc.) say how often something happens.

    ✓ Samantha is <u>*always*</u> on time for her Spanish class. (**Not**: Samantha *always* is on time for her Spanish class.)

    ✓ Visitors are <u>*sometimes*</u> unaware of the dangers of rip currents. (**Not**: Visitors *sometimes* are unaware of the dangers of rip currents.)

<u>Adverb Clauses</u>

Adverb clauses act as adverbs in a sentence—they modify verbs, adjectives, and adverbs. Like single-word adverbs, they can be recognized by the questions they answer. They tell:

- *When*
- *Where*

- *Why*
- *How*
- *Under what condition something happens*

They can also be recognized because they begin with subordinating conjunctions.

✓ *When I was a senior in high school*, I broke my arm playing basketball. (The adverb clause tells *when*.)

✓ I would help you *if I could*. (The adverb clause tells *under what conditions*.)

Adverb clauses can usually be moved around in a sentence. In the first sentence above, for example, the adverb clause can be placed at the end of the sentence without affecting its basic meaning.

✓ I broke my arm playing basketball *when I was a senior in high school*.

Notice that the adverb clause is followed by a comma when it comes at the beginning of a sentence; when it comes at the end, it is not preceded by a comma.

Practice Quiz

*Part 1: Choose the correct **adverb** for the following sentences.*

1. She quickly walked to the store.
   A. She
   B. quickly
   C. walked
   D. store

2. My mom and dad took us to eat yesterday.
   A. My
   B. took
   C. eat
   D. yesterday

3. Let's go to the mall later.
   A. Let's
   B. go
   C. later
   D. mall

4. The girls walked wearily down the road.
   A. girls
   B. wearily
   C. down
   D. road

5. Today, we are going to take a test.
   A. Today
   B. we
   C. are going
   D. test

6. Alex is _____ than Emma.
   A. smart
   B. smarter
   C. more smarter

D. smartest

7. The girls are _____ than the boys.
   A. prettier
   B. prettiest
   C. pretty
   D. more prettier

8. The questions are the _____ I have ever seen.
   A. hard
   B. harder
   C. hardest
   D. most hard

9. The dogs are playing _____.
   A. more joyfully
   B. most joyfully
   C. joyful
   D. joyfully

10. This test is _____ than that one.
    A. harder
    B. hardest
    C. hard
    D. more hard

For the answers, please go to page 126.

*Part 2: Read each sentence and identify the word as either an **adjective** or **adverb**.*

1. Wolves travel <u>far</u> when they hunt. (What part of speech is *far*?)
   A. Adverb
   B. Adjective

2. When they see prey, they move <u>near</u>. (What part of speech is *near*?)
   A. Adverb
   B. Adjective

3. New wolf mothers can be <u>unfriendly</u>. (What part of speech is *unfriendly*?)
   A. Adverb
   B. Adjective

4. Wolf puppies grow <u>quickly</u>. (What part of speech is *quickly*?)
   A. Adverb
   B. Adjective

5. The pups nearby always stay <u>close</u> to their mother. (What part of speech is *close*?)
   A. Adverb
   B. Adjective

6. Their prey takes them over the <u>far</u> horizons. (What part of speech is *far*?)
   A. Adverb
   B. Adjective

7. Wolves circle their prey and begin a <u>forward</u> movement. (What part of speech is *forward*?)
   A. Adverb
   B. Adjective

8. Their <u>hard</u> teeth make a loud sound. (What part of speech is *hard*?)

A. Adverb
B. Adjective

9. The small wolves chew <u>hard</u> on bones. (What part of speech is _hard_?)
   A. Adverb
   B. Adjective

10. They wolf failed at the hunt, but it was a <u>near</u> miss. (What part of speech is _near_?)
    A. Adverb
    B. Adjective

For the answers, please go to page 126.

Part 3: Choose the letter which has the correct answer.

1. Every sentence must have a(n) _____ and a verb.
   A. adjective
   B. adverb
   C. subject
   D. verb

2. The _____ is the word that tells what is being done.
   A. adjective
   B. adverb
   C. subject
   D. verb

3. A(n) _____ modifies (or describes) a verb, an adjective, or an adverb.
   A. adjective
   B. adverb
   C. subject
   D. verb

4. A word that modifies a noun is a(n) _____.
   A. adjective
   B. adverb
   C. subject
   D. verb

5. A(n) _____ answers the question "Who?" or "What?" before the verb.
   A. noun
   B. adverb
   C. subject
   D. verb

6. **What is the adverb in the following sentence?**

   The three quiet boys were sleeping silently.

A. three
B. quiet
C. silently
D. The

7. **What is the adverb in the following sentence?**

The very annoying squirrel ate my tennis shoes.
A. The
B. very
C. annoying
D. tennis

8. **What is the adverb in the following sentence?**

The Phonkadelics Jazz Band will play today.
A. Phonkadelics
B. Jazz Band
C. will
D. today

9. **What is the adverb in the following sentence?**

The handsome and charming man walked away.
A. away
B. charming
C. handsome
D. walked

10. **What is the adverb in the following sentence?**

Are you going to play now?
A. Are
B. you
C. going
D. now

For the answers, please go to page 126.

CHAPTER FIVE/THE ADJECTIVE.

In your writing, you will often want to modify (or describe) a noun or pronoun. The word you will use is an adjective. **Adjectives** usually answer one of the following questions:

- *How many?*
- *What kind?*
- *Which one?*
- *What color?*

✓ **How many?** <u>Many</u> students believe that the social security system will be bankrupt before they are old enough to retire. (<u>Many</u> modifies <u>students</u>.)

✓ **What kind?** <u>Blueberry</u> bagels gave us energy for our hike. (<u>Blueberry</u> modifies <u>bagels</u>.)

✓ **Which one?** <u>This</u> backpack was found in the cafeteria. (<u>This</u> modifies <u>backpack</u>.)

✓ **What color?** His <u>purple</u> socks did not complement his red suit. (<u>Purple</u> modifies <u>socks</u>.)

THE BREAKDOWN:

The adjectives in the sentences above came immediately before the nouns they modified. Some adjectives, however, came after linking verbs and describe the subject of the verb. Adjectives in this position are called **predicate adjectives.**

- ✓ We were surprised to learn that old pairs of American jeans in China are very _cheap._ (_Cheap_ is a predicate adjective because it comes after the linking verb _are_ and modifies the noun _pairs._)

- ✓ After waiting in the hot sun for three days, the refugees became _angry._ (_Angry_ is a predicate adjective because it comes after the linking verb _became_ and modifies the noun _refugees._)

Possessive pronouns (pronouns that show ownership such as _my, your, her, is, our,_ and _their_) are adjectives when they come before the noun.

- ✓ _our_ apartment.
- ✓ _their_ lunch break.

Spotting Adjectives

1. You can add '-er' and '-est' or _more_ and _most_ to adjectives.

   - ✓ _strong, stronger, strongest, eager, more eager, most eager_

2. An adjective will fill the blank in this sentence.

   - ✓ The cupboard is _empty._

3. Adjectives describe nouns and pronouns.

   - ✓ The _tired_ surfers paddled back to shore.
   - ✓ She is _proud_ of her degree in math.

4. Adjectives tells *how many, what kind, which one,* and *what color.*

✓ Ryan has *four* dogs, *three* cats, and a *dozen* goldfish.

✓ I have an *Ethiopian* pen pal and an *Ecuadorian* pen pal.

A special type of adjective is called the **article.** The English language contains three articles: *a, an* (used before words that begin with a vowel sound), and *the.*

✓ After *an* absence of sixteen years, Maricela returned to *the* city of her birth and *a* parade in her name.

Confusing Adjectives and Adverbs

Adjectives and adverbs are modifiers; they limit or describe other words.

✓ ***Adjective:*** *Moderate* exercise suppresses the appetite.

✓ ***Adverb:*** The surgeon *carefully* examined the sutures.

Many adverbs end in '*-ly*' (*hurriedly, graciously,* and *angrily*), but some of the most common do not (*here, there, now, when, then,* and *often*). Furthermore, some words that end in '*-ly*' are not adverbs (*silly, manly, chilly*).

Using Adjectives After Linking Verbs

The most common linking verbs are *be, appear, grow, remain, seen,* and the "sense" verbs (*feel, look, smell, sound,* and *taste.*) Words that follow such verbs and refer to the subject are adjectives, never adverbs. In the following sentences, the adjectives (called a predicate adjective because it follows the verb and modifies the subject) comes after a linking verb.

- ✓ Pablo's ideas are *exciting*. (*Exciting* modifies *ideas*.)

- ✓ Their wedding reception was *expensive*. (*Expensive* modifies *wedding reception*.)

The rule for deciding whether to use an adjective or an adverb after a verb is simple: if the verbs shows a condition or state of being, use an adjective after it.

- ✓ Mike's girlfriend appeared *nervous*.
- ✓ The math final seemed *easy*.

Most of us would not write or say, "This soup is warmly" or "She is beautifully." In both cases, we would instinctively use an adjective rather than an adverb. The choice is not so obvious with 'bad' and 'well'.

- ✓ **Nonstandard:** I feel *badly* about that. (*Badly* is an adverb and cannot modify the pronoun *I*.)

- ✓ **Standard:** I feel *bad* about that. (*Bad* is an adjective modifying *I*.)

- ✓ **Nonstandard:** That hat looks *well* on Maria. (*Looks* is a linking verb, and we need an adjective after the verb to modify the noun *hat*. *Well* is an adverb except when it means "to be in good health.")

- ✓ **Standard:** That hat looks *good* on Maria. (*Good* is an adjective modifying the noun *hat*.)

Choosing Adverbs or Adjectives

The choice of an adverb or adjective depends on the kind of verb in the sentence:

1. If the verb is a linking verb and you want to describe the subject, an **adjective** is correct.

2. If you want to modify a verb that shows action, an **adverb** is correct.

3. If you want to modify an adjective, an **adverb** is correct.

Adjectives usually come before the word they describe; when they follow the word they describe, they are set off with commas.

✓ **Usual order:** The loud and unruly crowd stormed the soccer field.

✓ **Inverted order:** The crowd, loud and unruly, stormed the soccer field.

Adjective Clauses

Adjective clauses modify nouns and pronouns in a couple sentences. Like all clauses, they have subjects and verbs. But, as dependent clauses, they must be attached to independent clauses to express complete ideas and to form grammatically complete sentences.

Most adjective clauses begin with the relative pronouns *which, whom, that, who,* and *whose,* but a few are introduced by *when, where, why,* and *how.* Adjective clauses usually immediately follow the noun or pronoun they modify.

✓ Any pitcher *who deliberately hits a batter* will be ejected. (The adjective clause modifies *pitcher.*)

✓ Drivers *whose cars are left unattended* will receive citations. (The adjective clause modifies *drivers.*)

> When using a string of adjectives, they should appear in a set order: size/shape + age + color + origin + material.

Reminders for Punctuating Adjective Clauses

1. If the adjective clause is essential to the meaning of the sentence, do *not* set it off with commas.

2. If the adjective clause is *not* essential to the meaning of the sentence, set it off with commas.

✓ Anne Frank's diary, *which she began in 1942*, was terminated by her capture and death in 1945. (The adjective clause provides nonessential information.)

✓ Anne Frank's diary was terminated by her capture and death in 1945. (Although the adjective clause has been removed, we can still identify the subject.)

Know How to Punctuate a Series of Adjectives

To describe a noun fully, you might need to use two or more adjectives. Sometimes, a series of adjectives requires commas, but sometimes, it doesn't. What makes the difference?

If the adjectives can pass one of two tests when you reorder the series or when you insert *and* between them, they still make sense.

✓ The *tall, creamy, delicious* milkshake melted on the counter.

✓ **Revised:** The *delicious, tall, creamy* milkshake melted on the counter.

The series of adjectives still makes sense even though the order has changed. And if you insert *and* between the adjectives, you still have a logical sentence.

✓ The *tall <u>and</u> creamy <u>and</u> delicious* milkshake melted on the counter.

Practice Quiz

Part 1: Choose the correct **adjective** for the following sentences.

1. Her hair is long and _____.
   A. curly
   B. happy
   C. slim
   D. late

2. He drives a bright red sports car. It's very _____.
   A. wild
   B. shallow
   C. fast
   D. tall

3. Today, the weather's going to be _____.
   A. hopeful
   B. warm
   C. blue
   D. urgent

4. This house is _____ and old.
   A. awkward
   B. electric
   C. large
   D. fat

5. I'm feeling really _____ today.
   A. late
   B. long
   C. happy
   D. round

6. The food at this supermarket is always _____.
   A. gentle

B. hopeful
C. empty
D. fresh

7. Her new husband is very _____.
   A. high
   B. smart
   C. urgent
   D. relaxing

8. Take care of this letter, it's _____.
   A. urgent
   B. round
   C. blonde
   D. fresh

9. I had a brilliant holiday. It was really _____.
   A. relaxing
   B. loving
   C. low
   D. straight

10. I have fallen in love with a _____ woman.
    A. closed
    B. beautiful
    C. wooden
    D. handsome

For the answers, please go to page 127.

*Part 2: Select the correct **adjective.***

1. Which word is an adjective?
   A. after
   B. pretty
   C. taste

2. Which word is an adjective?
   A. dirty
   B. ran
   C. away

3. Which word is an adjective?
   A. eat
   B. hot
   C. meal

4. Which word is an adjective?
   A. beautiful
   B. over
   C. wave

5. 'Lovely' is an adjective
   A. True
   B. False

6. 'Liquid' can be an adjective
   A. True
   B. False

7. Adjectives always come before the noun in the sentence.
   I.   True
   II. False

8. **How many adjectives are there in this sentence?**

   I thought the film was very long and boring.
   A. 1

B. 2
C. 3

9. **How many adjectives are there in this sentence?**

I need to find a new car that is less expensive to run than my old one.
A. 1
B. 2
C. 3

10. **How many adjectives are there in this sentence?**

You told me that the talk would be interesting.
A. 1
B. 3
C. 5

For the answers, please go to page 127.

Part 3: Choose the letter which has the correct answer.

1. Andrea had a _____ in her hair yesterday.
   A. nice yellow bow
   B. yellow nice bow
   C. bow nice yellow

2. She lost a _____ .
   A. small white cat
   B. cat small white
   C. white small cat

3. I bought _____ oranges.
   A. great some big
   B. big great some
   C. some great big

4. We met _____ people at the conference.
   A. very smart two
   B. two very smart
   C. very two smart

5. The clown was wearing a _____ hat.
   A. big green-yellow
   B. big green and yellow
   C. yellow and green big

6. The cookies that you _____ .
   A. smell delicious baked
   B. baked smell delicious
   C. delicious smell baked

7. Is it _____ ?
   A. cold getting outside
   B. getting cold outside
   C. getting outside cold

8. The course you are _____ .
   A. taking sounds interesting
   B. sounds interesting taking

   C. interesting sounds taking

   9. My uncle wore a _____ to the wedding.
      A. silk blue tie
      B. tie blue silk
      C. blue silk tie

   10. Have you met that _____ next door?
      A. cute boy new
      B. cute new boy
      C. new boy cute

For the answers, please go to page 127.

CHAPTER SIX/THE PREPOSITION.

What is a preposition?
connecting words.

Prepositions do not have any meaning or context in or of themselves. They exist only to show the relationships between other words. For this reason, they must be learned. Prepositions are words like *at, by, from,* and *with* that are usually followed by a noun or pronoun. (*at* home, *by* herself, *from* Oakland, and *with* you.)

THE BREAKDOWN:

The word following the preposition is called its **object**; the preposition and its object are called a **prepositional phrase**. A prepositional phrase can have more than one object and some prepositions are made up of more than one word.

- ✓ after *the meeting.*
- ✓ between *you and me.*
- ✓ through *the final week.*
- ✓ within *the hour.*
- ✓ without *a clue.*

Here are some of the most common prepositions. As noted above, some prepositions consist of more than one word.
Common Prepositions

about	above
according to	across
after	against
ahead of	along
among	around
away from	before
behind	below
beneath	besides
between	beyond
*but (when it means except)	by
concerning	despite
down	due to
during	except
for	from
in	in addition to
in front of	into
like	near
next to	of
off	on
onto	on account of
out	out of
outside	over
past	regarding

since	through
to	together with
toward	under
underneath	unlike
until	up
upon	with
within	without

But is very seldom a preposition. When it is used as a preposition, *but* means the same as *except*.

✓ Everyone ate frog legs _but_ Jamie.

But usually functions as a coordinating conjunction.

Tips: Recognizing Prepositions

1. A preposition is a word that will fill the slot in the following sentence.

"The airplane flew _____ the clouds."

✓ The airplane flew _above, below, beyond, under, around,_ or _through_ the clouds.

2. A preposition is a word that will fill the slot in the following sentence.

"A purse was lying _____ the street."

✓ A purse was lying _in, next to, alongside,_ or _beside_ the street.

Some prepositions, of course, will not fit either sentence, and they must be memorized.

<u>Prepositional Phrase as Fragments</u>

A prepositional phrase never contains a subject and a verb. Therefore, it can never stand alone as a sentence. The following sentences are followed by prepositional phrases high-power faking as sentences.

- ✓ **Fragment:** Some of the world's fastest boats raced for the cherished American cup. *Off the coast of Southern California.*

- ✓ **Fragment:** *After delaying it for several weeks;* Jeff finally began his term paper. *On the subject of religious cults in America.*

Because prepositional phrases are parts of sentences, the best way to correct this kind of fragment is to join it with the sentence to which it belongs.

- ✓ **Revised:** Some of the world's fastest boats raced for the cherished American Cup *off the coast of Southern California.*

- ✓ **Revised:** *After delaying it for several weeks,* Jeff finally began his term paper *on the subject of religious cults in America.*

Practice Quiz

Part 1: For each question, choose the best answer.

1. My best friend lives _____ Mack Road.
   A. in
   B. on
   C. at

2. I'll be ready to leave _____ about twenty minutes.
   A. in
   B. on
   C. at

3. Since he met his new girlfriend, Juan never seems to be _____ home.
   A. on
   B. in
   C. at

4. The child responded to his mother's demands _____ throwing a tantrum.
   A. with
   B. by
   C. from

5. I think she spent the entire afternoon _____ the phone.
   A. on
   B. in
   C. at

6. I will wait _____ 6:30, but then I'm going home.
   A. from
   B. at
   C. until

7. The police caught the thief _____ the corner of Tennyson and Hesperian.

A. in
B. at
C. from

8. My fingers were injured, so my sister had to write the note _____ me.
A. for
B. with
C. to

9. I am not interested _____ buying a new car now.
A. to
B. for
C. in

10. What are the main ingredients _____ this dish?
A. about
B. to
C. of

For the answers, please go to page 128.

Part 2: Complete each sentence with the correct preposition. Choose from the word bank below:

---
towards   underneath   until   up
with   within   without
---

1. During the earthquake, the ground _____ my feet began to shake.

2. When was the last time he went an entire day _____ a cigarette?

3. Lena likes to go shopping for clothes _____ her friends to get their advice.

4. The money that Laritha is saving will go _____ college for her kids.

5. People who live in southern and central Minnesota like to travel _____ north during the summer.

6. On the weekend, Loni doesn't wake up _____ 10 a.m. in the morning.

7. Is there a mosque that they can go to _____ the city?

8. The subway _____ the city can get people to their destinations very quickly.

9. This street goes _____ a very dangerous neighborhood.

10. It's probably going to rain, so don't leave _____ an umbrella.

For the answers, please go to page 128.

*Part 3: Fill in the blanks with suitable **prepositions**.*

1. Most people agree that kindergarten contributes _____ the child's mental development.

2. Since Monique was a year younger than her friends, she had a hard time keeping _____ with them.

3. In most countries, children start the primary school _____ the age of six.

4. Although he studied hard, he couldn't succeed _____ getting a high score in his test.

5. There are different sets of language learning sets available _____ all age groups.

6. All candidates are looking forward _____ the announcement of our test scores.

7. Since I will be busy _____ my homework, I don't think I will be able to go out tonight.

8. The students walk a mile to school, so they need to get up very early _____ the morning.

9. Since our school was next to our house, I used to come home _____ lunch time.

10. I was born _____ the 3rd _____ April.

For the answers, please go to page 128.

CHAPTER SEVEN/THE CONJUNCTION.

What is a conjunction?
a word that joins words or groups of words.

In a sense, **conjunctions** are like prepositions; they do not represent things or qualities. Instead, they merely show different kinds of relationships between other words or groups of words. There are two kinds of conjunctions you will need to recognize:

Coordinating conjunctions join words and word groups of equal importance or rank. You should memorize these coordinating conjunctions.

```
┌─────────────────────────────────────────┐
│       Coordinating Conjunctions          │
│                FANBOYS                    │
│                                           │
│    For   And   Not   But   Or   Yet   So  │
└─────────────────────────────────────────┘
```

THE BREAKDOWN:

The following sentences shows how coordinating conjunctions join single words and groups of words.

- ✓ Alexi speaks English *and* Spanish fluently. (*And* links two words.)

- ✓ Do you want wild *or* brown rice? (*Or* links two words.)

✓ Tao was born in Brazil, *but* he moved to the United States at the age of 4. (*But* links two independent clauses.)

✓ You should talk to a counselor, *or* you might take the wrong courses. (*Or* links two independent clauses.)

Coordinating conjunctions are used in compound sentences. Did you know that it used to be considered ungrammatical to begin a sentence with one of these words? But, this "rule" is no longer observed even by the best writers.

Some coordinating conjunctions combine with other words to form **correlative conjunctions.** The most common correlative conjunctions are *both...and, either...or, neither...nor,* and *not only...but also.*

✓ *Both* Ty Murray *and* Kristie Peterson are legends of professional rodeo.

✓ Ray will *either* go to summer school *or* work in his father's store.

Subordinating conjunctions, like coordinating conjunctions, join groups of words. Unlike coordinating conjunctions, they join unequal word groups or grammatical units that are "subordinate."

Some conjunctions like *after, before, for, since, but,* and *until* can also function as prepositions.

✓ The popularity of leisure suits declined *after* the presidency of Richard Nixon. (Preposition)

✓ Aisha sold her truck *after* she bought a minivan. (Conjunction)

✓ Jaime   bought   flowers   _for_ his   girlfriend. (Preposition)

✓ Jaime bought flowers_, for_ her knew his girlfriend was angry. (Conjunction)

✓ Every member of the General Assembly _but_ Cuba voted for the motion. (Preposition)

✓ Every member voted_, but_ Cuba demanded a recount. (Conjunction)

Compound Sentences

A **compound sentence** consists of two or more simple sentences (or independent clauses) containing closely related ideas and usually connected by a comma and a coordinating conjunction (_and, but, for, so, nor, or,_ and _yet_). Note how each of the following compound sentences consists of two independent clauses with related ideas joined with a comma and a coordinating conjunction.

✓ The average income of young American couples has increased_, but_ many of them cannot afford to buy a home.

✓ Vince offered to help cook dinner_, so_ Janet asked him to make the salad.

When these sentences are divided into halves, each half can stand as independent clause or simple sentence.

✓ The average income of young American couples has increased. Many of them cannot afford to buy a home.

✓ Vince offered to help cook dinner. Janet asked him to make the salad.

By combining sentences with commas and coordinating conjunctions, the results are longer, smother compound sentences. But remember, the independent clauses in a compound sentence must contain closely related ideas, and they are usually joined with a coordinating conjunction. Never try to combine two independent clauses with only a comma.

Most independent clauses are connected by coordinating conjunctions. You may never use a semicolon (;) to connect the clauses if the relationship between the ideas expressed in the independent clause is very close and obvious without a conjunction. In this case, the semicolon takes the place of both the conjunction and the comma preceding it.

✓ I love enchiladas and chile rellenos; they are my favorite kinds of Mexican food.

When using a semicolon, be certain that a coordinating conjunction would not be more appropriate. Using a semicolon in the following sentence would be confusing because the relationship between the two clauses would not be clear.

✓ **Confusing:** I have never played hockey; I like to watch hockey games on television.

By substituting a coordinating conjunction (and a comma) for the semicolon, you can make clear the relationship between the clauses.

✓ **Revised:** I have never played hockey, but I like to watch hockey games on television.

Punctuating Compound Sentences

If the independent clauses in a compound sentence are connected by a coordinating conjunction, place a comma in front of the conjunction. Do not try to combine independent clauses with only a comma—the result would be a comma-splice, a serious sentence error.

✓ **Comma-splice:** Calcium is important in one's diet, it is particularly important for pregnant women.

✓ **Revised:** Calcium is important in one's diet, and it is particularly important for pregnant women.

Do not place a comma before a coordinating conjunction if it does not connect independent clauses.

✓ **Nonstandard:** Herbs add flavors to salads, and are very easy to grow.

✓ **Standard:** Herbs add flavor to salads and are easy to grow.

✓ **Nonstandard:** My cousin Phil was born in Syracuse, but later moved to Buffalo.

✓ **Standard:** My cousin Phil was born in Syracuse but later moved to Buffalo.

In both sentences above, the conjunctions do not connect independent clauses, and therefore, they should not be preceded by commas.

Internal Punctuation

The Comma

The comma is the punctuation mark most frequently used inside sentences. As a result, many writers are uncertain concerning its proper use, and they sprinkle commas like #saltbae indiscriminately through their sentences. Do not use a comma unless you have a definite reason for doing so. The rules below will help you avoid cluttering your sentences with unnecessary commas while at the same time making sure you use them to make your meanings clear.

Use a comma to separate independent clauses joined by a coordinating conjunction (*and, but, for, not, or, so,* and *yet.*)

- ✓ Rhode Island is the smallest state, *and* Alaska is the largest.

- ✓ Her parents have been divorced for two years, *yet* they still remain friends.

You may omit commas before the conjunction if one or both independent clauses are short.

- ✓ Takisha left but Ramon stayed.
- ✓ I was exhausted but I couldn't sleep.

Note: Do not use a comma between two independent clauses that are not joined by a coordinating conjunction. This error creates a comma-splice. Use a coordinating conjunction or start a new sentence.

- ✓ *Comma-splice:* The chief mechanic examined the engine, his assistant checked the tires.

- ✓ *Revised:* The chief mechanic examined the engine, and his assistant check the tires. (**Or:** The chief mechanic examined the engine. His assistant checked the tires. *Or:* The chief mechanic examined the engine; his assistant checked the tires.)

Do not use a comma before a coordinating conjunction linking two phrases.

- ✓ *Nonstandard:* Shelly wrote a term paper on the history of jazz, and hip hop. (The conjunction *and* does not join two independent clauses.)

✓ **Standard:** Shelly wrote a term paper on the history of jazz <u>and</u> hip hop.

Use a comma to separate an introductory adverb clause from the main part of the sentence.

✓ When we visited San Francisco last summer, we went to a baseball game at AT&T Park.

✓ Although Japan lost WWII, the nation's economy recovered within a few years of its defeat.

Use a comma after a long introductory prepositional phrase and its modifiers.

✓ In preparing your annual report to the board of directors, be sure to include predictions for next year's sales.

Use a comma to set off an introductory participle phrase.

✓ *Remembering the promise made to his wife,* Maurice carefully kept a record of his expenditures and entered each purchase in his checkbook.

✓ *Pleased by the initial reaction from the customers,* the owner of the hardware store extended its sale another week.

Do not put a comma after participle phrases that are actually the subject of the sentence.

✓ **Nonstandard:** Playing golf once a week, was Carl's only exercise.

✓ **Standard:** Playing golf once a week was Carl's only exercise.

✓ **Nonstandard:** Reading about the lives of the Acadians, made me wat to visits Cajun country in Louisiana.

✓ **Standard:** Reading about the lives of the Acadians made me wat to visits Cajun country in Louisiana.

Use a comma to set off an introductory infinitive phrase unless the phrase is the subject of the sentence.

✓ To write a best-selling book, you must overcome tremendous obstacles.

▪ To win the jackpot in Las Vegas was his dream.

✓ To impress his future in-laws, was Marty's goals.

▪ To impress his future in-laws was Marty's goal.

Use a comma after an introductory request or command.

✓ *Remember*, tomorrow is the deadline for filing your tax return.

✓ *Look,* we've been through all of this before.

Use a comma to separate words, phrases, or clauses in a series unless all of the items are joined by 'and' or 'or'.

✓ She was young, attractive, and talented.
✓ She was young <u>and</u> attractive <u>and</u> talented.

✓ Ann made some sandwiches, Carolyn brought her guitar, and Tara furnished the soft drinks.

Use a comma to separate interrupting elements (words, phrases, and clauses) when they break the flow of a sentence.

✓ It is a fact, *isn't it*, that the spleen filters the blood?

✓ Jorge will stay, *if possible,* with his brother in San Jose.

Other interrupting elements (also called parenthetical elements or transitional expressions) include the following: *as a matter of fact, at any rate, for instance, nevertheless, of course, therefore, in my opinion,* and *on the other hand.* These and similar phrases are usually set off by commas when they appear in a sentence.

✓ My apartment, <u>on the other hand</u>, is situated on a lake.

✓ The store had three good reasons, <u>nevertheless</u>, for going bankrupt.

Use a comma to set off direct address and words like *please, yes,* and *no.*

✓ You should never wear a helmet, <u>Roxanne</u>, when you ride your motorcycle.

✓ Will you get off my foot, <u>please</u>?

Complex Sentences

Because their ideas can be shifted around to produce different emphases or rhythms, **complex sentences** offer the writer more variety than do simple sentences. Complex sentences are often more precise than compound sentences because a compound sentence must treat two ideas equally. Complex sentences, on the other hand, can establish more exact relationships.

An ***independent clause*** can stand alone and form a complete sentence. A ***dependent clause***, however, cannot stand alone. Even though it has a subject and a verb, it fails to express a complete thought. It must be attached to an independent clause in order to form a grammatically complete sentence.

You can recognize dependent clauses by the *kinds* of words that introduce them, making them dependent. The technical terms for these words are **subordinating conjunctions** and **relative pronouns.**

> ✓ *after* we reached our motel that night.
> ✓ *if* you speak a foreign language.

By adding an independent clause to each, you can change them into complete, grammatically correct *complex* sentences.

> ✓ After we reached our motel that night, we called our children.

> ✓ If you speak a foreign language, you have an advantage when applying for many jobs.

Note: *A dependent clause is often followed by a comma when it begins a sentence. If an independent clause comes first, no comma is needed.*

The following list contains words that most commonly introduce dependent clauses. Whenever a clause in a complex sentence begins with one of them (unless it is a question), it is a dependent clause.

Most Common Words That Introduce a Dependent Clause	
after	although
as, as if	as though
because	before
how	in order to
it	once
since	so that

than	that
though	unless
what, whatever	when, whenever
whether	which, whichever
while	who, whose, whoever
Whom	

Practice Quiz

*Part 1: Choose the **coordinating conjunction** that best expresses the relationship between the two ideas.*

1. Deserts are harsh and dry, _____ many plants grow there.
   A. for
   B. so
   C. yet

2. Pat looked at the antique rocker, _____ she couldn't afford to buy it.
   A. and
   B. but
   C. or

3. Constance might go to the library, _____ she might stay home.
   A. but
   B. so
   C. nor

4. Sue jogs every day, _____ she wants to stay in shape.
   A. but
   B. yet
   C. for

5. His shoes are worn, _____ he has no socks.
   A. for
   B. so
   C. or

6. Guy is a contractor, _____ he knows the construction business.
   A. so
   B. and
   C. but

7. Bill went to work, _____ he didn't punch in.
   A. or
   B. but
   C. so

8. My brother is in the play, _____ I want to attend the first performance.
   A. or
   B. so
   C. for

9. Annette couldn't go, _____ she was tired.
   A. nor
   B. yet
   C. for

10. Your niece and I went out to lunch, _____ we both ordered pasta.
    A. and
    B. or
    C. yet

For the answers, please go to page 129.

Part 2: Choose from among these **subordinating conjunctions** to complete each sentence:

although	as long as	because	even if
so that	unless	until	while

1. She has decided to move to Portland _____ there are more opportunities for employment in that city.

2. You can borrow my car _____ you agree to be very careful with it.

3. They'll have a good corn harvest this year _____ it rains a lot and prevents them from harvesting their crops.

4. Our neighbor is going to buy a gun _____ she can protect herself from intruders who break into her apartment.

5. _____ he can save a lot of money by taking the bus, Russ still drives his car into the city every day.

6. Ronald is going to finish his homework _____ it takes him all night.

7. My daughter can't wait _____ she gets her new bike.

8. Stay in the car _____ I go into the store. I'll be right back.

9. It's a good idea to go to college for four years _____ it's also possible to get a good job without a degree.

10._____ he's overweight, Dean eats a lot of food before he goes to bed. That's not healthy.

For the answers, please go to page 129.

Part 3: Choose the appropriate pair of **correlative conjunctions.**

1. _____ Alex _____ Carlos applied for the job.
   A. Whether...or.
   B. Both...and.

2. I found _____ my homework _____ my textbook under my bed.
   A. both...and.
   B. whether...or.

3. I can't decide _____ I should take French next year _____ take Spanish.
   A. either...or.
   B. whether...or.

4. _____ my brother _____ my sister can go to the game.
   A. Whether...or.
   B. Neither...nor.

5. _____ you clean your room _____ you will stay home this weekend.
   A. Either...or.
   B. Neither...nor.

6. Marissa found _____ the shoes she had lost _____ her favorite necklace.
   A. Neither...nor.
   B. Not only...but also.

7. _____ we go to San Francisco _____ New York for our holidays, I'll be happy.
   A. Whether...or.
   B. Either...or.

8. _____ did she do well on the math test, _____ she _____ got an 'A' on her social studies report.
   A. Either...or.

B. Not only...but also.

9. _____ I can go to the movies on Saturday, _____
    I can go to the mall.
    A. Either...or
    B. Neither...nor

10. Sorry, but I have _____ the money _____ the time
    to go shopping right now.
    A. Neither...nor.
    B. either...or.

For the answers, please go to page 129.

CHAPTER EIGHT/THE INTERJECTION.

What is an interjection?
a word that expresses emotion.

The **interjection** has no grammatical relationship with the rest of the sentence.

Mild interjections are followed by a comma.

- ✓ *No,* it's too early.
- ✓ *Yes,* that would be fine.

Strong interjections require an exclamation mark.

- ✓ *Wow!* My phone bill is huge!
- ✓ *Yo!* I'm over here.

THE BREAKDOWN:

An interjection is a word that expresses some kind of emotion. It can be used as filler. Interjections do not have a grammatical function in the sentence and are not related to the other parts of the sentence. If an interjection is omitted, the sentence still makes sense. It can standalone.

- ✓ *Oww!* That hurts.
- ✓ *Well,* I need a break.

When you are expressing a strong emotion, use an exclamation mark (!). A comma can be used for a weaker emotion.

Interjections do the following:

1. Express a feeling: *wow, oops, damn, geeze, oh.*
   ✓ *Oops*, I'm sorry. That was my mistake.
   ✓ *Geeze!* Do I need to do it again?

2. Say *yes* or *no*: *yes, no, nope.*
   ✓ *Yes!* I will do it.
   ✓ *Nope.* That's not what I want.

3. Call attention: *yo, hey.*
   ✓ *Yo*, will you throw the ball back?
   ✓ *Hey*, I just wanted to talk to you about our previous meeting.

4. Indicate pause: *well, um, hmm.*
   ✓ *Well*, what I meant was nothing like that.
   ✓ *Hmm.* You really need to be an adult.

Interjections are basically like emojis. One writer might write the sentence like this:

   ✓ This burrito is vegan! ☺

But, another writer might use an interjection to express that some burst of happiness.

   ✓ This burrito is vegan! Yum!

Good writers know that careful word choice can capture the same emotion and body language that the interjection communicates.

Practice Quiz

*Part 1: Select the **correct interjection**.*

1. An interjection is ___.
   A. an exclamation which shows thoughts or feelings
   B. a meaningless string of sounds
   C. the same as an adjective

2. Which of the following interjections is <u>NOT</u> an expression of surprise or wonder?
   A. Gee!
   B. Gosh!
   C. Boo!

3. You are vegan and you are offered a dish of raw meat. What do you think?
   A. Ugh!
   B. Hurrah!
   C. Yippee!

4. Somebody has just stepped on your toe. Which interjection would best fit the situation?
   A. Yoo-hoo!
   B. Ouch!
   C. Eh!

5. You are most likely to hear or use the interjection "boo" ___.
   A. at a theatrical performance
   B. while listening to a political speech
   C. on both of the above-mentioned occasions

6. ___, Mary! Come here! I want to talk to you.
   A. Oops
   B. Mmm
   C. Hey

7. Which of the following interjections is <u>NOT</u> used when watching a sad movie?
   A. Wahhhhhhh!
   B. Yay!
   C. Ahhhhhhh!

8. The interjection 'yesssssssss' implies _____.
   A. joy
   B. surprise or wonder
   C. irritation

9. Your children are making a lot of noise and you want to hear the news. How do you urge silence?
   A. Shh!
   B. Tut-tut.
   C. Ow!

10. Which of the following interjections is <u>NOT</u> used when cheering for a team?
    A. Rah!
    B. Yay!
    C. Yikes!

For the answers, please go to page 130.

Part 2: In the following sentences, identify the **interjection** and underline it.

1. Hi, I'm glad that you could make it to my party.

2. Wow! You look great tonight.

3. That was the best performance that I have ever seen, bravo!

4. I can't believe you broke my favorite toy, bah.

5. Hmm, I wonder where I put my keys and wallet?

6. Miners used to shout, eureka, when they struck gold.

7. "Shoo!" shouted the woman when she saw the cat licking milk from her cereal bowl.

8. I guess that's the end of the movie, darn.

9. Stop! You should always wear a helmet when riding a bike.

10. Yippee, I made this picture all by myself.

For the answers, please go to page 130.

Part 3: In the following sentences, write an appropriate **interjection** *in the space provided.*

1. _____, why didn't you hold the door for me?

2. _____, I'm so happy that you decided to visit this summer.

3. _____, it's not every day that you see a dog riding a skateboard.

4. _____! How can you possibly agree with that point of view?

5. He just cost us the game _____!

6. _____! You just gave me a great idea.

7. _____, that's a very large dog at the end of that leash.

8. I can't believe that I finally got an 'A' on a project, _____!

9. _____, my favorite author is doing a reading at the local library.

10. This is my first new car, _____.

For the answers, please go to page 149-150.

Answer Guide

How did you do?

Practice Quiz – The Noun

Part 1:

1. D
2. B
3. A
4. D
5. D
6. D
7. A
8. D
9. D
10. D

Part 2:

1. Common
2. Proper
3. Proper
4. Common
5. Proper
6. Proper
7. Proper
8. Common
9. Common
10. Proper

Part 3:

1. Plural
2. Plural
3. Singular
4. Singular

5. Plural
6. Singular
7. Plural
8. Singular
9. Plural
10. Singular

<u>Practice Quiz – The Pronoun</u>

Part 1:

1. She
2. He
3. I
4. They
5. Our
6. She
7. He
8. Me
9. Her
10. He

Part 2:

1. E
2. C
3. E
4. D
5. B
6. A
7. C
8. B
9. C
10. A

Part 3:

1. himself
2. herself
3. ourselves
4. yourself
5. myself
6. himself
7. itself
8. herself
9. yourselves
10. themselves

Practice Quiz – The Verb

Part 1:

1. C
2. B
3. A
4. C
5. C
6. B
7. B
8. B
9. C
10. A

Part 2:

1. B
2. A
3. A
4. A
5. B
6. B
7. B
8. B
9. B
10. B

Part 3:

1. B
2. B
3. A
4. B
5. A
6. A
7. B
8. C
9. A
10. A

Practice Quiz – The Adverb

Part 1:

1. B
2. D
3. C
4. B
5. A
6. B
7. A
8. C
9. C
10. A

Part 2:

1. A
2. A
3. B
4. A
5. A
6. A
7. B
8. B
9. A
10. B

Part 3:

1. C
2. D
3. B
4. A
5. C
6. C
7. B
8. D
9. A
10. D

Practice Quiz – The Adjective

Part 1:

1. A
2. C
3. B
4. C
5. C
6. D
7. B
8. A
9. A
10. B

Part 2:

1. B
2. A
3. B
4. A
5. A
6. A
7. B
8. B
9. C
10. A

Part 3:

1. A
2. A
3. C
4. B
5. B
6. B
7. B
8. A
9. C
10. B

Practice Quiz – The Preposition

Part 1:

1. B
2. A
3. C
4. B
5. A
6. C
7. B
8. A
9. C
10. B

Part 2:

1. underneath
2. without
3. with
4. towards
5. up
6. until
7. within
8. underneath
9. through
10. without

Part 3:

1. to
2. up
3. at
4. on
5. for
6. to
7. with
8. in
9. during
10. on, of

Practice Quiz – The Conjunction

Part 1:

1. C
2. B
3. A
4. C
5. A
6. A
7. B
8. B
9. C
10. A

Part 2:

1. because
2. as long
3. unless
4. so that
5. although
6. even if
7. until
8. while
9. even if
10. although

Part 3:

1. B
2. A
3. B
4. B
5. A
6. B
7. A
8. B
9. A
10. A

Practice Quiz – The Conjunction

Part 1:

1. A
2. C
3. A
4. B
5. B
6. C
7. B
8. B
9. A
10. C

Part 2:

1. <u>Hi</u> is the interjection and is used as a greeting.

2. <u>Wow</u> is the interjection and shows surprise.

3. <u>Bravo</u> is the interjection and is also used as a way to congratulate the participants.

4. <u>Bah</u> is the interjection and shows disappointment.

5. Hmm is the interjection and a verbalization of a mental process.

6. Eureka is the interjection and shows excitement.

7. Shoo is the interjection and is being used to verbally startle the cat.

8. Darn is the interjection and shows disappointment.

9. Stop is the interjection and ceases the forthcoming action.

10. Yippee is the interjection and shows excitement.

Part 3:

Answers will vary.